# RELIGION AND THE MODERN WORLD

## (A Study of the Philosophy of Dr. S. Radhakrishnan)

**Chikile Prema Kumar**

**AKANSHA PUBLISHING HOUSE**
**NEW DELHI-110002 (INDIA)**

**AKANSHA PUBLISHING HOUSE**
4649-B/21, Ansari Road
Darya Ganj, New Delhi - 110 002
Ph.: 23263193 / 9811582579 / 09435116718
Telefax: 011-23263193
Email: ektabooks@yahoo.com
www.akanshapublishinghouse.com

*Religion and The Modern World:*
*A Study of the Philosophy of Dr. S. Radhakrishnan*



First Published 2010
ISBN 978-81-8370-204-1



PRINTED IN INDIA

Published by Akansha Publishing House, New Delhi and Printed at Aryan Enterprises, Delhi.

*Dedicated to*
*My Father CHIKILE VISWAESWA RAO,*
*and*
*My Mother CHIKILE SIROMANI*
*with deepest respects.*

# Contents


*Foreword* ix

*Acknowledegements* xiii

1. Introduction 1
2. Religion: Meaning, Scope and Implications 9
3. Proofs for the Existence of God – Reason and Faith 34
4. Religion and Morality 63
5. The Concept of Evil 85
6. Religion, Society and Culture 108

*Summary and Conclusion* 131

*Bibliography* 145

*Index* 161

# Foreword

In India religious beliefs and practices have great impact on the personal lives of most people. Indian religions have deep historical roots that are recollected by contemporary Indians. Within India, are the vast majority of people engaged in ritual actions that are motivated by religious systems that owe much to the past but are continuously evolving. Religion is one of the most important facets of Indian history and contemporary life. A number of world religions originated in India, and others that started elsewhere found fertile ground for growth here.

Religion is based on the faith in the ultimate unity of man and God, the finite and Infinite. If a man is not essentially divine, all religion is impossible. The significance of religion lies in man's experience of the presence of God.

As an academic, philosopher, and statesman, Sarvepalli Radhakrishnan (1888-1975) is one of the most recognized and influential Indian thinker in academic circles in the 20th century. Throughout his life and extensive writing career, Radhakrishnan sought to define, defend, and promulgate the religion, a religion he variously identified as Hinduism, Vedanta, and the religion of the Spirit. He sought to demonstrate that the Hinduism was both philosophically coherent and ethically viable.

All religions upheld the moral virtues and teach the people to follow the path of truth and righteousness. This is needed to find the significance of religion and the vital role it plays in the modern world.

He often appears to feel at home in the Indian as well as the Western philosophical contexts, and draws parallels from both Western and Indian sources throughout his writings. Because of this, Radhakrishnan has been held up in academic circles as a representative of Hinduism to the West. Radhakrishnan believed that all religious teachings represented different paths to the same goal, and this was the basis of the movement founded in 1897 by Swami Vivekananda, whom Radhakrishnan acknowledged as a formative influence on his own work.

Philosophy of religion is the philosophical examination of the central themes and concepts involved in religious traditions. Philosophy of religion asserts the religious experience and tradition logically and establishes God as reality. Radhakrishnan holds that there can be no religious philosophy in the absence of religious experience. Radhakrishnan is explicit and emphatic in his view that religious intuition is a unique form of experience. Religious intuition is more than simply the confluence of the cognitive, aesthetic, and ethical sides of life. However vital and significant these sides of life may be, they are but partial and fragmented constituents of a greater whole, a whole which is experienced in its fullness and immediacy in religious intuition.

In this book Dr CH. Prema Kumar has devoted to the discussions of the nature and scope of philosophy of religion which mostly focused on the views of Radhakrishnan. The philosophy of religion has been discussed in the context of modern world, making reference to the thoughts and sayings of different thinkers. The book covers the foundations of religious belief, reasoning, revelation, faith, God, humanity, religious approach to evil and sin.

Dr. CH. Prema Kumar meticulously brings out the basic tenet of religion in their common base of equality, unity of humans, universality of religion and religious tolerance, secularism and truth. The present book is one of the important contributions to the study and understanding of philosophy of religion and covers an unbiased analysis of the issues of comparison. I congratulate the author for his contribution and wish him that he will continue the same spirit in philosophy of religion.

**S.D.A. JOGA RAO**

# Acknowledgements

I sincerely express my heartfelt feelings of appreciation and deep sense of gratitude to my Research Director, Prof. T. Christanandam, Head, Dept. of Philosophy & Religious Studies, Andhra University for his valuable suggestions, scholarly expositions and inspiration for the completion of this work.

I offer my humble regards to my parents Sri. Chikile Visweswararao and Smt. Ch. Siromani for their blessings. I am grateful to the Prof. L. Venugopal Reddy garu, Vice-Chancellor, Andhra University for his kind support. I would like to thank Prof. J.V. Prabhakara Rao, Principal, Colleges of Arts and Commerce for his kind blessings.

My profound thanks are due to Dr. Veerraju, Associate Professor and Deputy Director, Center for Religious Studies, Department of Philosophy & Religious Studies, Andhra University, for his concern for the completion of my work.

I am also thankful to all other faculty members—Prof. S. Satyanarayana, Director, Center for Religious Studies, Prof. P. George Victor, Director, Special Assistance Programme and Chairman, Board of Studies, Prof. Y.V. Satyanarayana, former Head of the Department, Prof. V.V.S. Saibaba, Dr. K.R. Rajani, Dr. S.C. Suguna Kumari, Dr. BVS. Bhanusree and Sri B. Ravibabu for their cooperation.

I express my sincere thanks to Prof. S.D.A. Joga Rao for having kindly consented to write the foreword. I owe a deep sense of gratitude to my family members, Ch. Indira, Ch. Anu Sree Prem, Ch. Rajakumar Raju, Ch. Neelima, Ch. Aruna Kumari, Ch. Ratnam Raju, Ch. Krishna Vamsi, Ch. Karishna Prudhevi, Ch. Prudhevi Raju, for their support.

Finally, I express my gratefulness to Shri M.P. Misra, Akansha Publishing House, New Delhi for evincing keen interest in the project and bringing out it elegantly in the present shape.

Visakhapatnam **Ch. Prema Kumar**

# 1

# Introduction

Religion is a universal phenomenon and it is a vital force in the human societies. The approaches of different religions to answer the ultimate questions are also different. The definitions that have been given and the theories that have been formulated reflect these differences. While some thinkers have defined religion covering some aspects; others have laid emphasis on individual aspect bypassing the social aspect of religion. No definition of religion is comprehensive and exhaustive. Perhaps there will never be a comprehensive definition covering all aspects.

Although religion is held to be a personal matter, it is a social reality. It embraces all the values, adding the peculiar characters of holiness to them. Religion recognizes the personality of God. It includes the values of Truth, Beauty and goodness overriding the individual or group interests.

Religion has made significant contribution to have moral basis for human life. All religions upheld the moral virtues and touch the people to follow the path of truth and righteousness.

There is need to find the significance of religion and the vital role it plays in the modern world. Religion constitutes an important part of human experience. The downfall of man owes its existence due to the moral degradation. Man has to liberate himself from the clutches of this world and pursue the higher values of life. He has to awaken from the deep slumber and become conscious of his real self.

The first chapter deals with the meaning, definition and scope of religion. The theories of religion, humanistic religion, primitive religion, aspects dealing with the philosophy of religion are also dealt in this first chapter.

In the words of Immanuel Kant "Religion is the recognition of all duties as divine commands."[1] Thus morality plays a vital role in religion. Religion and morality are inextricably bound up with each other.

The significance of religion lies in man's experience of the presence of God and his communion with Him and His love. Man has to share the social life as a religious ideal. He has to experience peace, joy and bliss in his communion with society. Man has to observe saintliness moral, goodness, truth in all aspects of his life. Man has to be prepared to suffer for a good cause. He has to aspire for the eventual attainment of spiritual perfection and happiness.

Religion is not same as philosophy of religion. If we examine the meaning of philosophy of religion it is not an organ of religion and it need not be undertaken from the religious standpoint. An agnostic, a theist and an atheist do philosophize about religion. It is an attempt to think critically and comprehensively about the religious beliefs. In the philosophy of religion clarity of statements, consistency of claims, adequacy of evidence and validity of argument are important. This chapter also deals with the theories of religion such as Animism conditioned by social environment. Another theory of religion naturalism is different from animism in which man personifies all objects of nature. Man's attitude towards natural phenomena forms the basis of this theory.

Radhakrishnan holds that there can be no religious philosophy in the absence of religious experience. Philosophy of religion asserts the religious experience and tradition logically and establishes God as reality. Philosophy of Religion rejects dogmatic method of theology and adopts a scientific view of religious experience. It is a rational assessment of religion and analyses the aspects of religion accessible to reason. Philosophy of religion tends to be critical in matters of religious faith. Religion in the philosophical context has to be related to a rationally coherent system.

When religion consists of actions that are humanly significant it is called humanistic religion. Humanistic religion cuts across the theistic and non-theistic religions. Humanism relies on reason and in the reliability of tested evidence. A humanist holds his religious faith on rational grounds. Religion does not deny the human dignity and human value. It is Radhakrishnan who has conceptualized religion and has given a humanistic interpretation of religion He says that there is no conflict between religion and a reasonable humanism.

The second chapter 'Proofs for the Existence of God' deals with different conceptions of the God's existence. God is responsible for the existence and fundamental character of the universe. In the words of Aristotle "God is the unmoved Mover." He is the Supreme Being the creator and sustainer of all things. God is held be aware of every thing and nothing is hidden from Him. He is omniscient and nothing remains outside His awareness. The existence of God and its significance is felt by making room for faith in human life.

While atheism believes in the nonexistence of God, agnosticism states that nothing is known or can be known of the existence of God. An agnostic has no sufficient reason either to affirm or to deny the existence of God. It means 'not knowism'. Skepticism doubts all accepted opinions.

Naturalism is a theory representing nature and it does not accept the supernatural or spiritual element.

St. Anselm's ontological argument to establish the existence of God is discussed in this chapter. God is a necessary being and self-existing. It is impossible to conceive of God as non-existing.

St. Thomas Aquinas has made an attempt to demonstrate the reality of God and offered five ways to prove the divine existence. He argues that there could not be a world without the idea of God unless there is God.

Rene Descartes' argument for the existence of God is discussed in this chapter. Immanuel Kant criticizes ontological argument of Descartes. Kant holds that existence is not a predicate.

The third chapter entitled ' Religion and Morality' deals with the relation of religion with morality. In the contemporary world situation the hardest problems being confronted by humanity are moral in nature rather than economic and political.

Morality deals with what is right or good in conduct. It considers the action of human beings with regard to their rightness or goodness. The term good signifies not something which is a means to an end but it self is taken as an end.

Social critics like Karl Marx view religion as an effort to support the moral norms, code of privileged and ruling groups. Religion deals with the most fundamental and difficult questions of the moral life.

The idea of God is the idea of perfect goodness. A religious believer feels that he obeys God by discharging his duty and by the cultivation of goodness. There is an intimate connection established between morality and religion and there can be no morality without religion.

The fourth chapter deals with the 'concept of evil', which assumes an important place in the human experience. Evil tends to be unpleasant, repulsive and offensive. Evil is not a problem to be solved but a mystery to be explored. Evil is not a problem outside man but a possibility within him. Evil includes the evil deed and its consequences with the element of decay, decadence, self-destruction etc. where as good has the elements of persistence, survival; permanence, value etc. The values like truth beauty and goodness endure eternally.

Suffering stands as a test to human lives. For religious people suffering comes as a special trial. Evil has a temporary and necessary place. Suffering is logically indispensable component.

The fifth chapter deals with 'Religion and Society.' Conditions prevailing in the modern society lack values of life. The society has deviated from the age-old traditions, value system and the established law and order. The ideas that have been regarded as valuable have lost their meaning. The modern society is rent because of misunderstanding internal differences and bitterness. The entire atmosphere is completely disturbed due to suspicion and uncertainty looming around with the fear of the future, and what it beholds.

Man has to find necessary remedies for the present, problem–ridden society. Though the modern man is the recipient of the benefits of Science and Technology, he is not fully aware of their bad effects and their catastrophic tendencies.

Science recognizes no boundaries in the socio - political spheres. The industrial revolution has affected economic relations. The progress and advancement of the modern world is measured in external and material terms. There is need to have regard for spiritual values, love of truth, and beauty, righteousness justice and mercy, sympathy with the down trodden and belief in the brotherhood of man. These qualities will save modern civilization, says Radhakrishnan. People should not be separated on the ground of religion, race nation or polity. They in no way contribute for the human unity and progress but retard it. Religion signifies faith in the absolute values and it shows a way of life to realize them.

Modern man is capable of evaluating the social and cultural roots of religion as well as the spiritual, ideational aspects of the cultural order. Religion is the greatest need of humanity. By no means can it be alienated from man. Religion has a cultural aspect and culture must be seen as a product of social organization.

Those who identify religion from the supernatural viewpoint, weaken the religion. The scientific influence may strengthen religion in the long run in the modern world.

All kinds of religion do not fit equally into the complex framework of modern societies. Some religions upheld faith in religion and others upheld reason in their constant search for truth to the full extent. For some, faith is fixed and final. Culture as a system of norms is inferred from the patterned actions of the members of the society. Society does not exist without culture. Culture is sustained through the human actions. Religion solves social problems and preserves the values. When social patterns change or a religion is transplanted into a new society, the changes that occur indicate the intimate connection established between religion and society.

Most of the cultural patterns, values and the nature of society are intimately connected with religion. The nature of relationship that exists between society and religion depends on the type of society. Religion provides the foundation for an orderly social life. Societies differ in their systems of morals as in other aspects of the social system. The established relation of religions of society to their particular system of morality has to be examined.

The higher value has to be set upon truth than upon any other principle. Human personality sustains because of the culture to which it belongs. Because of the cultural up rooting, structure of the human personality becomes weakened.

Culture is a way of life of the society. It is inclusive of the totality of values, norms, modes of thinking and the ways of acting shared by the number of people. Culture is the basic setting of the group in which organized activities are grounded.

Though the modern age has largely ceased to understand the meaning of religion, it is still in desperate need of that which religion alone can give.

> "The recognition of a transcendent Supreme, the freedom of the human individual as a manifestation of the Supreme and the unity of mankind as the goal of history are the foundations of the major religions. The religion of spirit reasserts these fundamental truths".[2]

There is no incompatibility between the findings of science and the doctrine of religion. The search for truth is their common goal though they have different ways of approach to it. Since God is Truth, the quest of truth is the quest of God. Man who makes the machine is greater than the machines.

Modern science enlarges the power of man to do evil as well as to resist evil. Humanity today faces a challenge of destiny. People can meet the challenge and build an international order, which allows freedom of development to the entire constituent states under a rule of law, which is enforceable by a world authority.

Religion is not irrelevant to human life. It has some guidance and helps to offer to a generation, which is perplexed at its failure to find satisfaction. Religion is now groping for light. Only a living faith in God will enable man to overcome the paralyzing sense of despair and create a more perfect society. Religion is the direct apprehension of the Supreme. It is the attaining of a state of illumination that awakens the real in man. It recreates Being itself. A truly religious man lives on the frontiers between the sacred and the secular between religion and politics, and between being and non-being. People are not called upon to get out of history and go to forest to lead lives of renunciation and resignation.

## REFERENCES

1. Immanuel Kant, *Religion Within the Limits of Reason Alone*, p. 142.
2. Dr. S. Radhakrishnan, *Recovery of Faith*, p. 186.

# 2

# Religion: Meaning, Scope and Implications

Religion is all-pervasive, and universal phenomenon in the human societies. Different religions attempt to answer the ultimate human questions in different ways. Religion is a vital force to the human lives. It has become both an individual as well as a social activity. In the human communities, the institutions of social life grow and develop in their own fashion. In the passage of time the community becomes adapt to the methods it follows.

Definitions and theories formulated reflect these differences. Some have defined religion covering some aspects and some have laid stress on individual aspect bypassing the social aspect of religion. No definition of religion is comprehensive and exhaustive. It is not easy to find a definition of religion in the substantive sense that accords general acceptance.

In the words of Paul Tillich:

> Religion is the state of being grasped by an ultimate concern, a concern, which qualifies all other, concerns as preliminary and which itself contains

> the answer to the question of the meaning of our life.[1]

Tillich gives a clue that enables to distinguish religious from non-religious beliefs objects and practices. Religion is conceived as a specific form of social consciousness. Its characteristic feature is a fantastic reflection in people's minds of external forces dominating over them. It is a reflection in which earthly forces assume unearthly forms. For Marxism and Leninism religion is a historically transient phenomenon of social phenomenon of social consciousness indicating the main factors that determine its existence at different stages of development of the society.

Religion is held to be a personal matter and a social reality. Throughout the history of humankind from the prehistoric times down to the modern times, religion has sought fellowship either by intensifying the existing social fabric, family, clean tribe, caste, local tribe, or natural community or by creating specifically religious communities within, above, or apart from other social and political groupings and institutions.[2]

The Oxford Dictionary defines religion as

> The belief in a super human controlling power especially in a personal God or Gods entitled to obedience and worship, the expression of this in worship, a particular system of faith and worship.

Religion ideally embraces all the values and adds the peculiar character of holiness to them.[3]

Religion is manifested as an element of human experience. The institutions, traditions, convictions and sacred writings are observable and open for examination. Most of the religions claim to be more than the collection of empirical data. Interior dispositions, values, fundamental orientations of life include the religious phenomena. Religion claims to be true. Religion implies an interpretation of the meaning of reality in terms of its value. It is reckoning with the possibility that something at the core of reality does respond and satisfy human demands for life and fulfillment of destiny.[4]

Religion characteristically is man's attempt to relate the disparate elements of his exterior and interior experience into a harmonious vision of the whole that will serve as a guide and a source of meaning for his understanding and his place in the world that enfolds him. World views are composed of all the cultural elements of man-science, art, philosophy, religion etc.[5]

The term religion indicates a bond of scruple uniting those who shared it closely to each other. Religion is a feeling of absolute dependence, and it is the organization of life. It is varied in form, completeness and clarifying in accordance with the environing culture. Ecstatic, transic and intense aesthetic experiences are found with in religious framework. The religious experience is religious precisely because it occurs in a religious context of thought, discipline and value.[6]

The development of the inner life in religion does not exclude the lower level of physical and material goods and they remain as the object of perfectly religious hopes to offer prayers for health, rain in the event of drought and sufficiency of food.[7]

## Meaning of Religion

Religion is personal and individualistic. Some people focus on the intellectual and emotional aspects of ethics and belief. Religion is conceived as a universal function of human societies. For many people religion is affair of the heart, so often inexplicable even to themselves, so colored by their own special feeling for the particular beliefs and ceremonies that they consider as sacred through long association. It is difficult of them to assume an objective and scientific stance.[8]

This world is a concrete spiritual world. The human experience reveals that personality implies much more. Human interest extends into the interest of other personalities implies much more. Human interest extends into the interest of other personalities to the past, future and beyond the apparent time limits of individual personality. It includes the striving for good conduct and search for truth that binds all. Truth, right and beauty are essentially one.

Religion is the recognition of all embracing personality of God, not merely theoretical but inclusive of the practical recognition of right, truth and beauty as of binding authority that is supreme overriding the individual or group interests.[9]

Religion is the vision of some thing that stands beyond and within and it is the passing flux of immediate things, it is something, which is real, but yet to be realized, something which is a remote possibility, excelling the existing facts, that gives meaning to all that passes, and cludes apprehension. It is something whose possession is the final good the ultimate ideal. It is an element in human experience, which persistently shows an upward trend. It renews its force and recurs with an added richness and purity of content. [10]

The primary meaning in religion is the experience of God to be in communion with him and with love and praise of him. The second meaning in religion is man's experience of himself as a mind. It has not to be identified with the body or any portion of it. The philosophy of religion affirms the whole experience of religion in which the mind is continuously present to itself.

The third meaning in religion lies in the acceptance and interpretation of nature as created by God. Nature is instrumental to the purposes of God, for men in the ideal. He reveals to them. Nature provides opportunities for enjoyment and God has given men the capacity for enjoyment.

The fourth meaning in religion lies in the sharing of social life, not primarily due to the result of biological process or for secular benefits but as a fundamental of the religious ideal.

The fifth meaning in religion is the experience of peace, joy and bliss in the communion of men.

The sixth meaning in religion lies in the acceptance of saintliness moral goodness, truth and beauty in all their forms as divinely intended for men Moral goodness depends upon the inner personal character and love for others. The seventh meaning in religion lies in the individual's consciousness of defect especially of sin with an awareness of the way of salvation. Sin is felt inwardly as an alienation from God. Social progress depends upon the spiritual regeneration of the individual.

The eighth meaning in religion is man's attitude towards suffering. What man sow's, he reaps. Suffering follows in reaping. Suffering is a challenge to the human spirit. Religion on the other hand promises salvation through redemption. This has to be attended through suffering. The ninth meaning in religion is the conviction of spiritual continuity beyond death. This is what is aspired and hoped for the faith in the eventual attainment of spiritual perfection and happiness. [11]

Religion is intimate and ultimate concern followed by convictions and activates dealing with the meaning of existence.[12] Religion is an attitude of the human will. It may not be used to signify a faculty of man but the active or functioning unity of the whole person. In some societies many religious attitudes find expression in other than religious forms. The relation between attitude and institution is more complex than they seem to suppose. Some sort of religious institutions is held to be essential if the religious attitude is to be effective in human society.

The terms such as the ultimate or the absolute with ultimate concern, absolutely honest mean unconditionally honest. Paul Tillich has given an explicit and a detailed philosophic treatment.

Paul Tillich states that:

> "The unconditional is a quality not a being. It characterizes that which is our ultimate and consequently unconditional concern, whether we call it God.... Or whether we give it any other name. It would be a complete mistake to understand the unconditional as a being the existence of which can be discussed. Unconditional is a quality, which we experience in encountering reality, for instance in the unconditional character of the voice of conscience, the logical as well as the moral.[13]

## Definitions of Religion

Religion in the past has been associated with the ideas of the supernatural and often it is based on the explicit beliefs about it. In the words of A.N. Whitehead, " religion is the art and the theory of the internal life of man so far as it depends on the man himself and on what is permanent in the nature of things."[14]

Religion is conceived primarily as a social fact as man cannot be abstracted from the society. "Religion is what the individual does with his own solitariness."[15] If man is not solitary, he can never be religious. In the words of Immanuel Kant "religion is the recognition of all duties as divine commands." [16]

According to Matthew Arnold religion is "Morality touched by emotion." Professor Taylor called religion "the belief in spiritual beings". In the words of Prof. Ames religion is " The pursuit on the part of the community, or the individual member of the community of what are thought to be the highest social values." Professor Stratton defines it as "man's whole bearing toward what seems to him the Best or

Greatest". Professor Lowie sees its essence in "sense of something is transcending the expected or natural, a sense of the extraordinary Mysterious or Supernatural." Salomon Reinach thinks it as "a sum of scruples which impede the free exercise of our faculties". Professor Hayden exalts it as "the co-operative quest for a completely satisfying life." According to George Bernard Shaw religion is " that which binds men to one another and irreligion that which sunders."[17]

Immanuel Kant says, "Religion consists in our recognition of all our duties as divine commands". Morality thus plays a very vital role in religion. Schleiermacher states that " Religion consists in our consciousness of absolute dependence on something which though it determines us, we cannot determine in turn." Here religion is considered to be predominantly as feeling. Hegel lays more stress on reason. He defines religion as "the knowledge acquired by the finite spirit of its essence as absolute spirit."

In the words of John Stuart Mill " The essence of religion is the strong and earnest direction of the emotions and desires towards an ideal object, recognized as of the highest excellence and as rightly paramount over all selfish objects of desire. Max Muller; a pioneer in the empirical study of religions wrote, that " Religion consists in the perception of the infinite under such manifestations as are able to influence the moral character of man." Rudolph Eucken conceives religion as "mystical experience in which the oppositions of life are transcended."

In the modern times religion is dealt not in ecclesiastical or theological context but in psychological terms. Many people mean religion as a psychological experience.[18] The psychological context has to descnibe religion in the most self-evident manner. It may well begin with behavior gradually penetrating as far as possible beneath the expression of spirit that animates it. The act of piety, which is a duty towards the Gods, then also loyalty to family and state with reverence for the laws. Thus the main phenomena of religion are covered by the word piety.[19]

Schleiermacher was the great interpreter of pietism who penetrated beneath external religious act to their source in feeling. His fundamental idea was that religion was a matter of feeling.[20]

## Theories of Religion

The theories formulated to explain the origin and growth of religion are numerous. In ancient India orthodoxy maintained that there was one inspired religion and all other religions are decadent form of it.

The theory animism is connected with the names of the sociologists – Sir Edward Taylor and Herbert Spencer. Animism is based on facts and inductions. The savage believes that what is active is alive. The living animal or material has within it the same sort of spirit which man recognizes in himself. So he treats the world with spirit inhabited objects. He thinks that when he dreams, his spirit goes out to perform the acts, which he imagines himself as doing in his dreams. Thereby he acquires the notion of a spirit independent of the body and attributes spirit and spiritual powers to other men, animals and objects as same as his own. When he sees a dead man apparently still alive in dreams, he infers that the spirit of the dead is still alive and that when he dies, he will be still alive. Because still living spirits may be malicious, the savage pacifies these potential forces by offerings ghostly, spirits are gradually endowed with more super human power. They have been revered as Gods. [21]

The second theory called naturalism is connected with the name of Max Muller. It is based on the theory of savages to fear and revere objects of nature that seem to them powerful. Such as a waterfall or thunderstorm or a majestic tree. To all these they attribute life and anthropopathy nature. In like manner, they revere venerable human phenomena, kings, and wizards. They identify the sky with people, the imagined kings and treat wizards as Gods of natural phenomenon. Man regards the sun as a great personage and the moon and the stars as mother and children Man personifies, all objects of nature and reveres what is awesome.[22]

A belief in ghosts is merely due to the belief in a continuation of life in a man. It is not a belief in higher beings surviving death. When they were alive they were not so capable in that condition.

**Evil Effects of Sin**

The word sin has a specific meaning in religion though widely used for wickedness. It goes beyond the naturalistic concept of immortality. It is not merely biological or with social import. In the religious context it is not to avoid suffering to be happy or to seek biological preservation and social harmony. Sin is man's inability to obey a categorical imperative. Man is in conflict with the principles and values that are absolute and violation of an order meant to be universal among men. Sin goes beyond the external conduct under terrestial conditions. Man is deprived of inner spiritual peace and satisfaction because of sin.[23] Moral rules have been famed as instrumental for intrinsic values. Man apprehends the absolute principles and values that are fundamental for religion but not out of the awareness of social mores and rules.

Religions are interested primarily in the choices relative to spiritual development and the efforts for the realization of the different aspects of the ideal. Man's existence in religion is not limited to terrestrial phenomena but as having a spiritual continuity beyond earthly conditions. He believes that some values he experiences in this life so far as he could realize help to endure in life after death.[24]

Religion in its developed forms may associate holiness and worship with physical power, goodness, and aesthetic beauty, intellectual truth or with any other human concern.[25] All religions include some system of beliefs; doctrines and dogmas designed to give intellectual expression to the commitment celebrated in its ritual. All religions include some systems of ethical obligations or code of conduct and social practices designed to relate them to the broader spheres of political, economic and social life. [26]

**Primitive Religion**

The religious feeling among primitive people is expressed primarily in feeling and in action and secondarily in the form of concepts and beliefs. Man attempts to come to grips with the mystery of life through gestures and acts. The beliefs, which explain or rationalize the gestures and acts, emerge later. [27]

The specific practices and beliefs of religion are claimed to be universally original Emile Durkheim states that the primitive people have exhibited behavior associated with an identification of the group with selected plants or animals. The tribal symbol is called after the name totem. The totem seems to be familiar to most people as typical objects of primitive societies. Durkheim holds that totem symbolizes both cosmic power and the power of the group relationships. It is ultimately society itself to which man is related in religious belief and behavior. Human society is conceived as God.[28]

The distinction between "I and We" seems to be vague among the primitive people. The simplest human societies are so complex that the individual member is radically dependent on other members for the fulfillment of basic human needs. It is group rather than the individual that develops customs laws, rites and ceremonies, which make individual life meaningful. Primitive man calls attention to the "we consciousness and its significance for even the most highly individualistic, of civilized culture". [29]

Sir James George Frazer made a monumental study of primitive religion. He concluded that totemic and other practices of primitive people may have either or two family distinct general aims namely the bending of cosmic and social powers to the will of the individual or group or bending of the will of the individual of group to the powers recognized to be superior. Frazer held that former type of activity should be properly labeled as magical and the latter type is distinctively religious. Magical practices aim to control or export the natural and social forces for individual and social ends.

The closer investigation of primitive cultures reveals that most primitive people used to live in a world of intangible spirits which serve to naturalize man and humanize nature in order to bridge the gap between the human and the nonhuman, the animate and the inanimate in primitive thinking. The belief in spirits and the behaviour associated with it is called animism, which means soul. The whole idea of a spirit-centered reality constitutes a primitive worldview. Individually baffling mysteries could be clarified. There by wind seems to be mysterious basically related to life itself the breath of life, which moves in and out of the body. The mystery enveloping the wind and breath becomes identical with the mystery of life and death.[30] The primitive man believes that the breath of life is not limited to living bodies but it is rather pervasively present in all nature and the world itself is alive.[31]

The phenomena of nature evoked feelings of awe and wonder among the primitive people. This stimulated in them some sort of religious feeling and made them act. The natural phenomena such as water, fire, sun and moon have been worshipped by the people and even in the modern time, they remain as examples of religious expression. In the passage of time, as the human civilization advanced religion and religious activities have been associated with certain rites ceremonies, dogmas and superstitions. All these acts have had their basis on belief or faith.

**Philosophy of Religion**

Philosophy of Religion is not an organ of religious teaching. It need not be undertaken from religious standpoint. The atheist who does not believe in the existence of God and the agnostic who is not sure of the existence of God and a theist who believes in the existence of God could philosophize about religion. Philosophy of religion does not constitute a branch of theology, which rationally analysis religious faith, but it is a branch of philosophy. It studies the concepts and propositions related to theology, phenomena of religious experience, and activities of religious worship on which theology rests.[32]

> The philosophy of religion is, among other things an attempt to think critically and comprehensively about these religious beliefs and claims clarity of statements, consistency of claims, adequacy of evidence, validity of argument and comprehensiveness of generalization are matters of primary concern for the philosophy of religion as it seeks to examine the definitions and theories of religion.[33]

According to Radhakrishnan, philosophy of religion is a religion that comes to an understanding of itself. He holds that there can be no religious philosophy without religious experience. It is an attempt to organize and unify the data of religious experience. It needs carefully to be distinguished speculative theology from that of dogmatic theology. Speculative theology proceeds from general principles by means of dialectic and arrives at the conclusion that God is a possibility. Philosophy of religion proceeds from religious experience and tradition and asserts logically that God is a reality. Dogmatic theology restricts itself to the exposition of one set of experiences recorded in a particular age and country but philosophy of religion takes into account the different types of religious experience of all ages and countries.

Radhakrishnan says, that

> "Philosophy of religion rejects the high a priori road of speculative theology and the apologetic method of dogmatic theology and adopts a scientific view of religious experience and examines with detachment and impartiality the spiritual inheritance of men of all creeds and even of those who have none. Such an examination of the claims and contents of religious consciousness, which has for its background the whole spiritual idealism which is opposed to the disintegrating forces of scientific naturalism on the one hand, religious dogmatism on the other.[34]

Philosophy of religion is not itself a part of the religious realm but it is related to it is as the philosophy of law is related to the realm of legal phenomena and to judicial concepts and reasoning's. The philosophy of religion is thus related to the particular religions and theologies of the world in the manner the philosophy of science is related to the special sciences. Philosophy of religion analyzes the concepts such as God, salvation, holiness, worship, creation sacrifice, eternal life etc., and determines the nature of religious utterances in comparison with those of everyday life, scientific discovery, and morality. etc. [35]

The philosophy of religion has to make an investigation on the nature of religion in general and deal with the main ideas of the different religions. There have been a great variety of anthropological, sociological, psychological, naturalistic and religious theories of the nature of religion as it has been viewed by the anthropologist, sociologist, and psychologist, naturalist in different ways.[36] As a result there has been no commonly acceptable viewpoint of religion.

The aim of philosophy is to understand and discover the truth to the satisfaction of reason. In the philosophy of religion this aim is directed towards religion. Religious ideas to some extent are conceptual with logical significance and establish their truth or falsity through questioning. In the philosophy of religion, rational truth contained in religion is found. The truth contained in religion does not have in the rational content discovered. The philosophy of religion makes an effort to discover the aspects accessible to reason.[37]

In the words of Clayton Fever

> The task of philosophy of religion, which is to examine, criticize and assess the validity of at least the human elements in religious experience, is thus two fold. On the one hand, it has the function of interpreting, evaluating and integrating the data of religious experience, as these are manifest in human behaviour. On the other hand, it must appraise the adequacy of the religious expression as an interpretation of reality.[38]

The philosophy of religion is considered to be a subdivision of philosophy dealing uniquely with religious aspects of philosophy, knowledge and value, aspects such as God, the immortality of the soul, mystical experience and the priorities and obligations of the religious man. [39]

Brightman holds that almost all great religious thinkers of Christianity, Judaism, Islam, Brahmanism etc., have been far more than dogmatic expounders of an uncivilized faith though religion is thought to preclude philosophical investigation. Some philosophers have related their tenets to human experience as a whole and subjected them to radical criticism.

Brightman says

> Religion is not abstract idealism, it is concrete and practical. It asserts that ideals are not only

> abstractly valid in the Platonic kingdom of ideas, but also that they are to some extent realizable and realized in the world of actual existence. The belief that ideals are valid but are not potent in actuality is the position of an idealistic pessimist... religion requires the conservation of values. Religion therefore can be understood only when the philosophical problem of the relation of ideals of to existence is thought through.[40]

Philosophy of religion has had its beginning with religion as distinctive, to be differentiated from the intellectual grasp of truths and from moral and aesthetic experiences. Philosophy of nature starts from the sense experiences of the physical world and moral philosophy from moral judgments and philosophy of religion begins with religion in its own intrinsic nature.

Philosophy of religion attempts to give a comprehensive view of religion. Some of the religions in reality are in emotional attitudes and some, anticipated and striven for, are expressed in ideals. In the past the philosophies paid insufficient attention to the empirical facts of the physical world. All religions stress on future attainment as expressed in their ideals.[41] The fundamental problem of philosophy of religion is to turn the relation from value experience to sense experience.[42] The criterion of coherence implies that no truth can be completely tested or proved until all truth is known. The facts, which are not yet known, may be required for the modification or rejection of any known truth. All the results offered by all other proposed tests, revelations or insights must come before the tribunal of the whole mind and its grasp on experience as a whole. This alone justifies or verifies a scientific hypothesis or a religious faith.[43]

The practical consequences of ideas are facts, must be considered. If a belief is not tested, in experience, it is blind and useless.[44] Philosophy of religion is critical in its perspective in the matters of religious faith - in matters of intimate and ultimate concern. So it has to be familiarized with the information in the field of anthropology, history, psychology and carryout investigation in these fields as far as possible. The method employed has to be constructive and critical to gether facts about religion and it has to be objective, open and dispassionate.[45] Religion in the philosophical context has to be related to a rationally coherent system [46]

## Religion and Reason

Immanuel Kant says that when a person comes to know of something as his duty before accepting it as a divine injuction is natural religion. On the other hand he who interprets the natural religion alone as morally necessary as his duty can be called the rationalist. If he denies the reality of all supernatural divine revelation, he is called a naturalist. If a person recognizes revelation but assets that to know and accept it as real is not a necessary requisite to religion he could be named as pure rationalist. When the person holds that belief is necessary to universal religion, he could be named as the pure super-naturalist in matters of faith.[47]

A rationalist restricts himself within the limits of human insight. He will not dogmatize. He does not contest either the inner possibility of revelation in general or the necessity of revelation as a divine means for the introduction of a true religion. For the matters of this nature no person could determine through reason.

The pure rationalist and the super-rationalist depending on their claims of reciprocity in the matters of faith can have a unique true religion. A religion with respect to its characteristics that are capable of being shared widely with others can be of two kinds. It could be a natural religion of which every one can be convinced through his own reason or a learned reason through which one can convince others through his own the agency of learning. Depending on the capacity of general dissemination, the essential character of the Universal religion could be constituted and it ought to be binding upon every man.[48]

Kant holds that such a religion could be natural and at the same time revealed. Man could and ought to have discovered it of themselves through the use of their reason. A revelation there of at a given time and in a given place might well be wise and very advantageous to the human race. When religion introduced has been made known publicly, everyone can convince himself of his own reason of his truth. Thereby the religion is objectively natural religion though subjectively, it has been revealed.[49]

Even if a religion is revealed, it must contain certain principles of natural religion. It is only through reason that could add revelation to the concept of a religion. Therefore the revealed religion is looked upon as a natural one. The complete religion could be presented to all people comprehensibly and convincingly through their own reason.[50]

## Religion and Humanism

Among all the ideologies underlying the modern world, the principle of secularism seems to be more universal. Secularism is not atheism. Framework does not prevent the possibility of contact between man and God. It does not prevent the possibility of contact between man and God and it does not obviate the possibility of a religious belief. It is not the Denial of the existence of God, but rather the denial of his central role as a constructive factor in human reality that characterizes the secular attitude. [51]

No religion can afford to deny the worth and dignity of man mor deprecate the indissoluble bonds between man, his fellow man and mankind that became the seat of the intrinsic value of life. Humanism in the modern age that upholds human dignity, rights and values could not ignore human transcendence.[52] Humanism is stated to be a polite term of atheism. It is a religion of humanity.

Radhakrishnan holds the similar view. He says

> If the humanists regard the enhancement of personality as the chief end of life, our life cannot be reduced to either physical manhood or economical well being or instructed mind or sensitive conscience. We cannot live up to the full height of our potential being without drawing upon the deeper resources of spirit. The roots of man's being are in the unseen and eternal and his destiny is not limited to the duration of his life on earth.[53]

Radhakrishnan holds that there is no conflict between religion and a reasonable humanism. In his view. point the truly religious act in this world, the inner feeling of the relation between God and man is bound to issue in the service of humanity while what matters is works or fruits of religious life, its social productivity, the most efficient servants of society are those who cultivate anxiously the interior life. A religion wherein man is the center but not God can never be a strong one. [54]

In the words of Dr. S. Radhakrishnan

> There is no conflict between religion and a reasonable humanism. The truly religious act in this world; the inner feeling of the relation between God and man is bound to issue in the service of humanity. While what matters is works or fruits of religious life, its social productivity, the most efficient servants of society are those who cultivate anxiously the interior.A religion whose center is man and not God is never a strong one. [55]

Humanism is related to value religion on the other hand relates value to reality. Humanism is right when it exalts man as mind, but it is not a mere body or mind but spirit as well. So humanism can do duty for an adoring life, which is identified with the mind of God and manifests itself in service and self.[56]

Julian Huxley maintains that theistic religions usually adopt the hypothesis of revelation and they assert that truth has been revealed in a set of commandments, which are God given, or in a holy book. So the beliefs of theistic religion inevitably tends to be authoritarian, rigid and resist to change.

When the religious change is inevitable in the changing human world, it does occur but it often involves merely the substitution of one authoritarianism for another.[57] Huxley treats all the religious systems as social organs whose function is to adjust man and his destiny. He maintains that the previous system could not perform this function properly as the previous age has no sufficient knowledge to construct an adequate picture about the destiny of man.[58] Julian Huxley regards religion as applied spiritual ecology, which has to attempt to deal with the relation of mankind with the rest of external nurture, the relation of man's individualized self with the rest of his internal nature and the relation of individual men and women with other men and women and with their communities.[59] Man has to change his traditional outlook and outdated ideas about religion. His emerging religion therefore must also learn how to be an open and self-correcting system like that of science.[60]

Humanism believes that the task of religion has to bring about the integration of human life and man has to take steps in this process. He has to be integrated as an individual and as a member of society. He has to find his place in the larger universe. Man as a measure of all things is inclusive of religion and it is a human problem.[6]

Julian Huxley emphasizes the need for the emergence of a new religion without giving amy vent to a belief in the supernatural God. For him religion is an organized system of ideas and emotions relating to man and his destiny.[62]

**Humanistic Religion**

The religious humanists regard the universe as self-existing but not created. Man as a part of nature has emerged as the result of the continuous process. Religious humanism maintains that all associations and institutions exist for the fulfillment of life.[63] The humanists hold fast to the principle that the truest religion is that which issues and fosters the best life. Some humanists hold that humanism as religion.[64] But Blackham denies humanism as religion and says that humanism is not religion but it is more than morals without religion.[65] A humanist holds religion conditionally on rational grounds retaining his primary faith in reason.[66]

Eric Fromm a well-known psychoanalyst attempts to review the types of religion. He brings out the essential element in authoritarian religion. It is a religious experience in which man is surrendered to a power transcending him. The characteristic or this religion is marked by man's original sin and his disobedience. The deity is conceived as omnipotent or omniscient; and man is conceived as powerless and insignificant. Man gains grace or help from the deity by his complete surrender. In his act of surrender he loses his independence and integrity as an individual but gains the feeling of being protected by an awe-inspiring power of which he becomes a part. "In authoritarian religion God is a symbol of power and force. He is supreme because He has supreme power and man in juxtaposition is utterly powerless."[67]

Humanistic religion on the contrary keeps man and his ability at the center. Man must develop his power of reason in order to understand himself his relationship to his fellow beings and his place in the universe. Truth has to be recognized as per his limitations and his potentialities. Religious experience in this kind of religion is to have the experience of oneness with the all based on one's relatedness, grasped with thought and love. Man has to achieve the greatest strength, and the virtue of self-realization but not powerlessness or obedience.[68]

In humanistic religión God is the image of man's higher self, a symbol of what man potentially is or ought to become but in authoritarian religion God is the sole possessor.[69] Religious formulations and symbols are attempts to give expression to certain kinds of human experience.[70] Humanism has become a religion for some people as it provides answers to the question of the meaning of life but it is not concerned with the supernatural or life after death.[71]

**Religion and Agnosticism**

Religion insists on an organic connection between the world of nature and the world of values and delivers mankind from isolation and transience. It deeper than intellect and reestablishes the vital relationship in operation between man and nature.[72]

Agnosticism is a doctrine that denies completely or partially the possibility of knowing the Universe. An agnostic accepts that there is a reality behind the phenomena. He holds that there is something behind the phenomena though one cannot be certain of its nature. One cannot be certain that he could not know any more if that of which he admittedly knows so much unknowable. While to be ignorant is not the special prerogative of man but to know that he is ignorant is his special privilege. It sets limits to ones ignorance and knowledge. It is vain to urge men to turn away from the pursuit of the real.[73]

The Buddha's attitude seems to have been that of complete agnosticism. In the West, agnostic monism tends towards the belief that death is the extinction of individual life. The belief in the transmigration of souls does not establish scientific evidence.[74]

## Religion and Mysticism

Mysticism is a religious and idealistic view of the world based on the belief in the supernatural. It owes its origin in secret rites conducted by the religious societies of ancient orient and occident. It is a secret hidden or inexplicable matter. It is conceived as a religious truth divinely revealed transcending human reason. The rituals conducted are to establish contact between man and God or some other mysterious being. Communion with God is established through the experience of ecstasy or revelation. It is a belief in intuitive apprehension of God.

Mystics and mysteries are commonly classed together, so much so mystics could be called the adepts of the system of worship though not identified with religion. Religion is made to take its rise in mystery. So mystery has to be considered an inevitable stage in the development of religion. Mystery leads in two directions - towards ever increasing light and clearness and other towards increasing darkness and confusion.[75]

In the modern period mysticism has found a rich source of inspiration in physical nature. Above all, it is the disposition to see in the common affairs of life so as to transform them. They reflect the glory of God and bind the co-workers with one another and with Him in a spiritual unity. This may be stated to be the practical mysticism of the modern world.[76] Religious practices are not superstitions or artificial inventions. They are the spontaneous expressions of human nature as many found in secular life.[77] Religious practices and organizations of religious communities give an indication of the prominent character of religion.[78]

## REFERENCES

1. Paul Tillich, *Christianity and the Encounter of the World Religions*, p. 4.
2. Miracea Eliade, *Encyclopedia of Religion*, p. 307.
3. P. Atkin Son Lee, *Groundwork of the Philosophy of Religion*, p 80.
4. J. Clayton Fever [ed], *Religion in Philosophical and Cultural Perspective*, p.6.
5. *Ibid*, p.18.
6. Miracea Eliade, *op.cit.*, p.286.
7. *Ibid.* p.288.
8. Elizabeth, K., Nothingham, *Religion a Sociological View*, pp. 3-4
9. William Ralph Inge. *Freedom Love and Truth*, pp. 47.
10. *Ibid.* p. 51.
11. Alban G. Wildgery, *What is Religion*, pp. 291-295.
12. John A Hutchison & James Alfred Martin, Ways of Faith, p. 9.
13. Paul Tillich, *The Protestant Era*, p. 32.
14. George L., Abernethy, *Philosophy of Religion*, p. 50.
15. *Ibid.*
16. Immanuel Kant, *Religion within the Limits of Reason Alone*, p. 142.
17. Harry Emerson Fosdick, *As I See Religion*, p. 8.
18. *Ibid.*, p. 10.
19. Atkin Son Lee, *Groundwork of the Philosophy of Religion*, p. 23.
20. *Ibid.*, p. 23.
21. E. Washburn Hopkins, *Origin and Evolution of Religion*, p. 3.
22. *Ibid.*, p. 4.
23. *Ibid.*, pp. 178-80.
24. *Ibid.*, p. 273.

25. John A. Hutchison James Alfred Martin, Jr. *Ways of Faith*, p. 29.
26. *Ibid.* p. 36.
27. Emile Durkheim, *The Elementary Forms of Religious like*
28. John A Hutchison & James & Alfred Martin, *Ways of Faith*, p. 20.
29. *Ibid.* p. 21.
30. *Ibid.* p. 25.
31. *Ibid.* p. 25.
32. John Hick, *Philosophy of Religion*, p. 2.
33. George L. Abernethy, *Philosophy of Religion*, p. 1.
34. S. Radhakrishnan, *My Search for Truth*, p. 85.
35. John Hick, *Philosophy of Religion*, p. 35.
36. *Ibid.*, p. 35.
37. George L. Abernethy, *Philosophy of Religion*, p. 130.
38. J. Clayton Fever, *Religion in Philosophical and Cultural Perspective*, p. 6.
39. Rem. B. Edwards, *Reason and Knowledge*, p. 3.
40. Daniel J. Bronstein, *Approaches to the Philosophy of Religion*, pp. 3-4.
41. Alban G. Widgery, *What is Religion*, p. 235.
42. Daniel J. Bronstein, *Approaches to the Philosophy of Religion*, p. 12.
43. *Ibid.* p. 15.
44. *Ibid.* p. 14.
45. John A. Hutchison, *Ways of Faith*, p. 45.
46. *Ibid.* p. 46.
47. Immanuel Kant, *Religion With in the Limits of Reason Alone*, p. 143.
48. *Ibid.* p. 143.
49. *Ibid.* pp. 143-146.
50. *Ibid.* p. 144.
51. Nathan Rotensstich, *Humanism in Contemporary Era*, p.22.

52. Radha Kamal Mukerji, *The Ways of Humanism*, pp. 16-34.
53. Dr. S. Radhakrishnan, *Idealistic View of Life*, p. 65.
54. *Ibid.* p. 56.
55. *Ibid.* p. 56.
56. *Ibid.* p. 56.
57. Julian Huxley, *New Bottles for New Wines*, p. 283.
58. *Ibid.* p. 288.
59. Julian Huxley, *The Humanist Frame*, p. 43.
60. *Ibid.* p. 43.
61. *The Humanist*, 1946, pp. 1660-61.
62. *The Humanist*, 3rd Edition, 1952, Vol, XII No. 3, p. 202.
63. *The Humanist*. Vol-XII. 1953. p. 60.
64. Reuben Abel, *Humanist and Pragmatism*, p. 274.
65. H.J. Block ham, *Humanism*, p. 43.
66. *Ibid.* p. 28.
67. George L. Abernethy, *Philosophy of Religion*. p. 83.
68. *Ibid.* pp. 83-84
69. *Ibid.* p. 88.
70. *Ibid.* p. 9.
71. Ram B. Edwards, *Reason and Religion*, p. 7.
72. S. Radhakrishnan, *A Idealistic View of Life*, p. 45.
73. *Ibid.*, p. 47.
74. Atkin Son Lee, *Ground Work of the Philosophy of Religion*, p. 127.
75. *Ibid.* p. 178.
76. *Ibid.* p. 179.
77. Alban G. Wildgery, *What is Religion*, p. 204.
78. *Ibid.* p. 233.

# 3

# Proofs for the Existence of God – Reason and Faith

The word God is used as simply equivalent to the object of highest devotion. God is responsible for the existence and fundamental character of the universe. Aristotle used the word. "Unmoved mover" though he insisted that this cosmic keystone was not concerned about the universe.

In the theistic sense God is accepted as the Supreme Being and object of ultimate valuation. In order to specify the prime characteristics essential to theistic use of the term "God" three major topics God as being, God as thinking, and God as willing may be dealt with.

God of theism is considered to be actual. The theists use God as the reality ultimately responsible for the being of the entire universe. He is held to be the creator of all things. He is the maker and sustainer of all things. Thereby the theistic God is comprehensively relevant to the believer's life. His role as contemporary sustainer is distinguishable from the deistic view, which is based on reason and the creator, is no longer engaged actively with his handiwork. His power or being is grounded in his immanence.

God has the creating and sustaining power of being for the universe. His sovereignty must be absolute. The creator stands in a different relation to his created work. From that any created thing can possibly stand to any other created thing. He has the power to make and unmake. He has the limitless ability to sustain or to destroy. Even lesser power is inclusive of the power of being. No external limits would be imposed upon the powers or the ground and sources of all things.[1] God is held to be aware of every thing and He is not unconscious. Perfect knowledge must be ascribed to God. His knowledge is not partial. He is omniscient; nothing known can remain outside his divine awareness.[2]

God exercises His will. He is not without aim. It is possible to conceive a supremely actual creator sustainer who has perfect awareness of himself and the universe. He has no particular preference as far as the course of events are concerned. This conception may sound high and noble. It does not qualify as a theistic view of God. Theistic traditions ascribe purposive and valuing capacities to their object of highest devotion. While some courses of God's actions are in accordance with His will and policies, some events would be in violation of that will. God's goodness is upheld, as flawless God is unique. He is the only God absolutely good all knowing and unconditionally actual.[3]

## The Judaic Conception of God's Existence

The *Old Testament* constitutes the sacred writings of Judaism and the New Testament, the sacred writings of Christianity. According to Judaism and Christianity, God is an unlimited being His divine attributes or characteristics are so many in which the infinite divine reality exists. Among these attributes that those could be placed, the scholastics called deity being from oneself unusually called as "self existence".

In the Old Testament, the Hebrews believed in only one God. As a great contemporary. Biblical scholar says "Hebrew monotheism arose through the intuitive perception that a God. Who is righteous first and the last must be as universal as righteousness itself."[4] The monastic faith finds its primary expression in the commands and prayers, psalms prophecies; parables and teachings of the Bible. All these have been philosophically elaborated and defined through the long history of Christian thought. Judaism is the religion of the Jews. It came into its full existence after the destruction of the temple in 70 AD. Judaism has been fully developed by 500 AD.

**Existence of God**

Atheism is a belief according to which God does not exist and there is no God of any kind (not Judaism). Agnosticism states that nothing is known or can be known of the existence or nature of God or of anything beyond material phenomena. An agnostic has no sufficient reason either to affirm or deny the existence of God. It means literally "not know - ism "skepticism is inclined to doubt all accepted opinions. The soundness of accepted ideas and facts have been questioned. Naturalism is a theory that represents nature. It excludes the super natural or spiritual element. It is an action based on natural instincts. In the naturalistic theory, every expect of human experience including man's moral and religious life could be adequately described and accounted for in terms of his existence. Monotheism as a doctrine is based on the belief that there is only one God. It is one God-ism. God is the Supreme Being who is personal and moral. He seeks a total and unqualified response from his human creatures.

God is conceived as infinite and unlimited. Paul Tillich holds that one should not even say that God exists, as it is a limiting statement about Him.

Paul Tillich says

> Thus the question of the existence of God can be neither asked nor answered. If asked it is a question about that which by its very nature is above existence and therefore the answer-whether negative or affirmative – implicitly denies the nature of God. It is as a theistic to affirm the existence of God as it is to deny it God is being it self; not a being.[5]

God has primordial nature and a consequent nature, which is conscious It is the realization of the actual world in the unity of his nature through the transformation of his wisdom. While the primordial nature is conceptual, the consequent nature is the weaving of God's physical feelings upon his primordial concepts. One side of God's nature constitutes his conceptual experience, which is the primordial fact in the world limited by no actuality, which it presupposes. So it is infinite devoid of all negative pretensions. Conceptual experience can be infinite and it belongs to the nature of physical experience. An actual entity in the temporal world is to be conceived as originated by physical experience. God is to be conceived as originated by conceptual experience with his process of completion motivated by physical experience initially derived from the temporary world.[6]

God must be conceived as a reality, which is genuinely related to the human life in the world. The people and their various actions make a difference as to its actual being. The significance of human life has to be a supremely relative reality; God must be enjoying real internal relations of all the human actions and be affected by them in his own actual being.[7]

Existence properly functions as an abstract constant always implies actuality, as an abstract variable hence to say that any thing exists requires that the variable actuality have some specific value.[8]

In the nature of God, permanence is primordial and flux is derivative from the world. In the nature of the world flux is primordial and permanence is derivative from God. The world's nature is a primordial datum for God. God's nature is a primordial datum for the world. Creation achieves the reconciliation of permanence and flux when it reaches the state of its final term, which is everlastingness. [9]

Philo of Alexandria, influenced by the Greek thought argues from the existence of the human mind to the Mind of the universe. Philo states that no one could look upon statues or paintings without thinking at once of a sculptor or painter. No body could see cloths or ships or houses without getting the idea of a weaver or a shipwright or a house builder. When a person enters a well-ordered city in which the argument for civil life is admirably managed, what else will he suppose than those good rulers who directed the city. ?

When he comes to the truly Great city, of this world and beholds hills and plains teeming with animals and plants. spring fed or winter torrents, the yearly seasons passing through, the heavenly bodies, fixed the planetary system and the whole firmament revolving in rhythmic order, necessarily gain the conception of the Maker. The highest knowledge and art shown in the universe wrought by absolute perfection has the conception of the existence of God.[10]

People are led to have complete conviction and in any event they have very good reasons for believing in God. In the atheistic view, the existence of the universe is a sheer unexplained brute fact. The purposiveness in nature is only apparent Moral standards are found only in man. Yet men obey them even when they seem detrimental to their own interests. The religious experience of mankind is a vast delusion. But once it is acknowledged about God, there is an explanation despite the terrible problem of evil. The idea of God is conceivable as perfect being in the mind as there is such a Being. (The ontological argument). The world is there because God is there. (The cosmological argument) There is evidence of design in the universe because there is really a Mind that designs. (The teleological argument) The moral standards in God (The moral argument). Man has religious experience because he approaches his Maker. (The argument from religious experience) All this makes theism the most reasonable way to explain the world.[11]

J.N. Findlay defines the idea of God as the idea of the adequate object of religious attitude. In the religious attitude one tends to humble himself before some object; accepts it wholly and devotes himself to it with unquestioning enthusiasm the religious attitudes presume superiority in their objects and reduce themselves to a feeling attitude of nothingness.[12]

### St. Anselm's Argument

The subject of the existence of God is a problem revolving around the theistic proofs and it has become a center of debate since the time of Plato. Whether these arguments succeed in establishing their conclusion or not and are of any positive religious value are disputed questions.[13]

Anselm's argument hinges upon the definition of God as "something than which nothing greater can be conceived". The ontological argument for the existence of God was at first developed by Anselm. He was one of the Christian church's most original thinkers.

Some have undertaken the arguments for the existence of God in order to remove the unnecessary obstacles to belief and others rely on arguments for the existence of God to provide the foundation for the belief in God to be based.

The argument of St. Anselm hinges upon the definition of God as "something than which nothing greater could be conceived." By the word greater St. Anselm means superior or more perfect but not spatially larger.[14]

His argument is that it is incoherent and self-contradictory to think of such a being as not existing for a nonexistent entity or a nonentity is not the most adequate object of worship and no more perfect can be conceived other than.[15]

God gives understanding to faith. No other being greater than God can not be thought of, Man understands what he hears and what he understands is in his understanding even if he does not understand that it exists.[16]

Anselm in his discussion makes no appeal to any facts about the nature and existence of the world. It is an a priori proof, which has its basis in the pure reason without any appeal to human experience about the world. [17]

**The Ontological Argument**

The ontological argument finds in the very idea of God the proof His existence. The thought of God in the mind demonstrates His being. If such a being did not actually exist, one could conceive of another being who does exist who would be more perfect. The existence being one of the attributes, it must be ascribed who is an absolutely perfect or infinite Being, who is thought to be absolutely perfect. If He does not exist, He would actually lack one of His essential attributes.[18]

Man as a spiritual being, his whole conscious life is based on a universal consciousness, an Absolute spiritual life, which is not a mere subjective notion or conception, but which carries with it the proof of its necessary existence or reality.[19]

The ontological argument for the existence of God was first developed by Anselm one of the most original thinkers. Anselm begins the Christian concepts, of God into the formula "a being than which nothing greater can be conceived. 'By the word greater Anselm means more perfect, rather than specially bigger', The idea of the most perfect conceivable being is different from the idea of the most perfect being that there is Anselm holds that the ontological argument could not be formed upon the notion of the most perfect being that there is. Though it is true by definition that the most perfect being that there exists, Anselm held that there is no guarantee that this being is God. Consequently, instead of describing God as the most perfect being that there is; he describes God as the being who is so perfect that no more perfect could even be conceived.[20] Anselm distinguishes between some thing existing in the mind alone and its existence in reality as well. If the most perfect conceivable being exits only in the mind, there should be the contradiction that it is possible to conceive yet a more perfect being namely the same being existing in reality and also in the mind. So the most perfect conceivable being must exist in reality and in the mind.

Anselm says

> Therefore, if that than which a greater cannot be thought is in the understanding alone, this same thing than which a greater cannot be thought is that than which a greater can be thought. But obviously this is impossible without doubt, therefore, there exist, both in the understanding and in reality, something than which a greater cannot be thought.[21]

Anselm states that God is defined in such a way that it is impossible to conceive of him not existing. He is a necessary being and self-existing. God in his infinite perfection is not limited in or by time the possibility of his ever coming to existence and his ever ceasing to exist are alike excluded. His non-existence is rendered impossible.[22]

Anselm refers to the Psalmist's fool who says that " there is no God" His heart. He holds that even if such a person possesses the idea of God as the greatest conceivable being when the implications of this idea are removed, one could see that such a being must actually exist; unless the most perfect being exists, He cannot be conceived.[23]

**Proofs for the Existence of God**

These proofs of the existence of God possess real significance. These proofs are simply expressions of the impossibility of resting in the finite. They are with that of the implicit reference to an Infinite and Absolute Mind. If taken in their natural order, the proofs of the being of God are the their following.

1. The Cosmological

2. The Teological

3. The Ontological.

The Cosmological argument is from the contingency of the world. The contingent world exists. The world of human immediate experience is contingent. So an absolutely necessary Being exists. Proceeds from the thought that the world as presented to the human experience in it has no substantiality or independence. Its existence cannot be explained from itself. The human mind finds it necessary to have a Being who is self dependent and substantial.[24]

If the form of the idea of causality is taken, it is the argument that whatever does not exist necessarily exists only through another being as its cause and that again, if itself not necessary through another as an infinite regress of causes and effects is unthinkable. The mind is compelled to stop short and place at the head of the series First cause; a Being who is its own cause that exists unconditionally and necessarily.[25]

When began an infinite or absolute cause, one may conclude to finite effects but the process cannot be reversed. From a finite or contingent effect one could infer is a finite or contingent cause; or an endless series of such causes. If the mind cannot rest in the false infinity, one can try to stop the indefinite regress and assert at any point of it a cause, which is not an effect, which is its own cause or which is unconditioned and infinite. The conclusion that could be drawn is purely arbitrary.[26]

The idea of an infinite negates and annulus's the finite because it is insufficient. But it is true and necessary as a stepping-stone towards a higher idea. The infinite that one reaches by the denial of the finite is not held to be the true finite for the true Infinite must explain the finite instead of annulling it. The mind in the search of an absolute reality, seeks it in the mere negation of the unreal and transient when one does not find the real or substantial in the world of immediate experience, he naturally looks for it in that which is the opposite, or contradictory to that world. An Infinite, which is the negation of the finite, or the contingent, is not truly infinite or absolute.[27]

The world of experience may be insubstantial and phenomenal. In the reality which one seeks beyond the world; there must be something that accounts for it and does not merely annul it.[28]

In the idea of an all-wise Creator or Designer, the conception of a cause follows which is not merely to correlate an effect outside itself but which is self-conscious and self determined before it determines anything else.

God is thought of as a being, self-conscious and self-contained who freely or out of his own will and pleasure creates and workout certain purposes or ends in the world. The existence of an infinite explains about itself and the existence of the finite world. It conceives the relation of God to the finite world as that of creator and contriver. The mind goes beyond the alternatives of contingent and necessity. In the idea of an all-wise Creator or Designer, man has the conception of a cause. It is self conscious and self-determined. God is thought of as a Being who is self-conscious and self-contained. He freely of His own will and pleasure, creates and works out certain purposes or ends in the world. Since these ends are indicative of skill, contrivance, ingenious adoption of means to the accomplishment is a foreseen plan, God is inferred as infinite power with infinite wisdom and fore thought.[29]

God is not a mere abstract Infinite confined to the mere barren self- sufficiency but an infinite by its very nature must reveal itself in and communicate itself to a world of finite existences the creation of the world is grounded in the nature of God.

## St. Thomas Aquinas' Conception of the Existence of God

St. Thomas Aquinas attempts to demonstrate the reality of God. He offers five ways to prove the divine existence. Unlike the ontological argument, which focuses attention on the idea of God, he made a beginning from some general feature of the world in order to prove the existence of God. He argues that there could not be a world with this particular characteristic unless there is also the ultimate reality, which is called God.[30]

St. Thomas while referring to the proof for the existence of God, argues that motion or change means the reduction of a thing from a state of potentiality to that of action He holds that a thing cannot be reduced from potentiality to act except under the influence of an agent. Every thing being moved must be moved by another. He states finally, that in order to avoid an infinite regress in the chain of movers, the existence of a first unmoved mover must be admitted and all understand that as God Himself.[31]

While in the first proof St. Thomas Aquinas considers things as being acted upon and as being changed or moved in the second proof, he considers them as active agents and efficient causes. He states that there is a hierarchy of efficient causes. A subordinate cause is dependent upon the cause above it in the hierarchy and concludes that there must be a first efficient cause which all call "God".[32]

In the third proof Aquinas starts from the fact that certain things come into existence and perish. He concludes that from this it is possible for them to exist or not to exist and they do not exist necessarily. He asserts that it is impossible for things, which are of this kind to exist always. Which is capable of not existing at some time does not exist. If all things are of this kind, at sometime there would be nothing. Aquinas supposes for the sake of argument, the hypothesis of infinite time. His proof is designed to cover this hypothesis. He does not believe in the impossibility of infinite time. He says that if time is infinite and if all things are capable of not existing, the potentiality would be fulfilled in infinite time inevitably and then there would be nothing.[33]

The fourth argument is admitted to be difficult to grasp. Aquinas holds that there are degrees of perfections in things. Different kinds of finite things possess different perfections in variable limited degrees. He argues that if there have been different degrees of perfection like goodness; there is a supreme good to which other good things approximate and all limited degrees of goodness are caused by the supreme good. Since goodness is a convertible term with being, a thing being good in so for as it has being, the supreme good is the Supreme Being. He is the cause of being in all other beings. So there is something, which is the cause of the being and goodness and of every perfection in all other things, and this is called "God".[34]

St. Thomas Aquinas writing two centuries after Anselm rejected the ontological argument. St. Thomas Aquinas holds that the existence of God is self-evident. The knowledge of God is naturally implanted in all. So the existence of God is self-evident. When the nature of a whole and of a part is known, it is recognized that every whole is greater than its part. As soon as the significance of the name of God is understood, it is once seen that God exists. When the name is signified, then nothing greater could be conceived. That which exists actually and mentally is greater than which exists only mentally. As soon as the name of God is understood, it exists mentally. It follows that it exists actually.[35]

The existence of truth is self-evident Who ever denies the existence of truth grants that truth does not exist. If truth does not exist, the proposition, truth does not exist is true. If anything is true. There must be truth God is truth itself. "I am the way the truth and the life. (John 16 – chapter. 6th Verses.) Therefore, the existence of God is self-evident.[36] The existence of truth in general is self-evident but the existence of fundamental (Primal) truth is not self-evident.[37]

The existence of God cannot be demonstrated for it is an article of faith. What is of faith cannot be demonstrated as demonstration produces scientific knowledge. If the existence of God were to be demonstrated, this could only be done from his effects. But His effects are not proportioned to Him since He is infinite and His effects are finite. There is no proportion between the finite and infinite since a cause cannot be demonstrated by an effect not proportioned to it, the existence of God cannot be demonstrated.

When an effect is better known than its cause, one could proceed to the knowledge of the cause from the effect. From every effect the existence of its cause can be demonstrated as long as its effects are better known because every effect depends upon its cause. If the effect exists the cause must pre-exist. Hence, the existence of God in so far as it is not self-evident can be demonstrated from those of the effects, which are known. The existence of God and the truths about God knowable by natural reason are not articles of faith.[38] When the effects are not proportioned to the cause, no perfect knowledge of that cause can be obtained. From every effect, the existence of the cause can be clearly demonstrated. So the existence of God can be demonstrated from his effects but God cannot be known perfectly as He is in His essence.[39]

## The Existence of God in Five Ways

The existence of God can be proved in five ways. The argument from the motion can be described as the first way. It is certain and evident to the human senses that in the world certain things are in motion. Whatever is moved is being moved by another. Nothing can be moved it is potentiality to that towards which it is moved. A thing moves as long as it is in action. Motion is nothing but the reduction of something from potentiality to actuality. Nothing can be reduced from potentiality to actuality except by something in a state of actuality. It is not possible that the same thing should be at once in actuality and potentiality in the same respect but in different respects. It is impossible therefore that in the same respect and in the same way a thing should be both mover and moved. So whatever is moved must be moved by another. Therefore God exists as that other.[40]

The second way is from the nature of efficient cause. In the world of sensible things, an order of efficient causes could be found. In no case is a thing found to be the efficient cause as it would be impossible to be prior to itself. On the other hand in efficient causes it is not possible to go on to infinity. It is because that in all efficient causes following in order, the first cause is the intermediate cause. The intermediate is the cause of the ultimate cause whether the intermediate cause is several or one only. To take away the cause is to take away the effect. So if there is no first cause among efficient causes, there will be no ultimate nor any intermediate cause. If it is in the case of efficient causes, it is possible to go on to infinity and there will be no first efficient cause. There will not be an ultimate effect and any intermediate efficient causes.[41]

The third way is out of possibility and necessity In nature things; they are possible and not possible as they are found to be generated and to be corrupted. Consequently, it is possible for them to be and not to be It is impossible for these to exist always. If any thing cannot at one time there is nothing in existence. If this is true, there would be nothing in existence. It is because that which does not exist begins to exist only through something already existing. Therefore if at a time nothing existed, it would have been impossible for any thing to have begun to exist and even now nothing would be in existence, which is absurd. So not all beings are merely possible. But there must exist something, the existence of which is necessary. Every necessary thing has its necessity caused by another or not. It is impossible to go on to infinity in necessary things which have their necessity caused by another. It has been already proved in regard to efficient causes. So the existence of some being having of itself its own necessity and not receiving it from another but rather causing in others their necessity, which is known to be God.[42]

The forth way depends upon the graduation to be found in things. The human beings differ in degree of goodness, truth and nobility. The maximum in any genus is the cause of that genus. Fire, which is the maximum of heat, is the cause of all hot things. Therefore there must also be something, which is to all beings the cause of their being, goodness and every other perfection, which is called God.[43]

The fifth way is taken from the governance of the word. The things, which lack knowledge as natural bodies, act for an end. Their acting always in the same way so as to obtain the best result. They achieve their end designedly. What ever lacks knowledge cannot move towards an end unless it is directed by some being endowed with knowledge and intelligence similar to that of an arrow directed by the archer. So an intelligent being exists by whom all natural things are directed to their end and, being is called God.[44]

## Rene Descartes' Arguments for the Existence of God

As a result of the vast respect accorded to Aquinas's criticism, the ontological argument has been dropped out of discussion by the end of 13th century until the middle of the seventeenth century. It was Rene Descartes who provided the new formulation of the ontological argument and there have been a great deal of discussions in the modern period.

The ontological argument is not the only theistic proof that Descartes used. He formulated an argument to God as the cause of our idea of him. It is an argument similar to the ontological. In that it starts from the concept of God as the infinitely perfect being. But it is like the cosmological argument. In depends upon the principle. On the one hand the argument is claimed to be a necessary prelude to the ontological argument. It guarantees that the properties, which are necessarily affirmed of anything by the human minds, must belong to it on reality. It is a premise which the ontological argument when applied to the theistic concept as one includes the property of existence.[45]

Rene Descartes was called the father of the modern philosophy. He reformulated the ontological argument of Anselm and thereby attracted wide spread attention to it. He gave a new direction in his attempt to prove the existence of God. He brought to the forefront about ontological argument. It is based on the assumption that existence is a property or predicate. He treats existence as a characteristic and the possession of it is open to inquiry. The essence of each kind of thing includes certain predicates. His ontological argument claims that existence must be included among the defining predicates of God. He held that just as the fact that its internal angles are equal to two right angels is a necessary characteristic of a triangle, so also existence is a necessary characteristic of supremely perfect being. Since a triangle without its defining properties would not be a triangle, God without existence would not be God. The important difference is that in the case of the triangle one cannot infer about the existence of any triangle for the reason that the existence is not of the essence of triangularity. Where as in the case of a supremely perfect being, one could infer existence for existence sake is an essential attribute without which no being would be unlimitedly perfect.[46]

But Cartesian version of the ontological argument has been challenged later at two levels by the great German Philosopher, Immanuel Kant. He accepted Descartes claim that the idea of existence belongs analytically to the concept of God, as the idea of having three angles belongs analytically to the concept of a three sided plane figure. He stated that in each case the predicate is necessarily linked with the subject. But Kant in his reply, stated that it does not follow from this that the subject with its predicates actually exists. If there is a triangle, it must have three angles, and if there is a perfect being, he must have existence is analytically true.

Kant rejected the basic assumption of Descartes at a deeper level. He stated that the assumption like triangularity is a predicate, which something can either have or lack and it may in some cases be analytically connected with a subject.[47]

Immanuel Kant was a critique of the ontological argument in its Cartesian form. The basic contention of Kant is some times expressed in the slogan that "existence is not a predicate." It has been reformulated in the century by Bertrand Russell. Kant holds that existence is not a property

The concept of an absolutely necessary being is a concept of pure reason. A mere idea of objective reality is very very far from being proved. Reason requires to prove it. The idea instructs in regard to a certain unattainable completeness. There have been so many obstacles on the way to be faced in the matter of the inference from a given existence to some absolutely necessary being which seems to be imperative and legitimate.[48]

Kant maintains that both the cosmological and teleological arguments depend ultimately on the ontological argument which is held be the wider argument from perfection. It is within the framework of a concept of being. None greater can be conceived which attributes to the necessary being the properties of omnipotence omniscience and all embracing reality.[49]

The universe envisaged by the theist, differs in its totality from the universe as envisaged by the atheist. This difference does not however from the present standpoint with in the universe, involve a difference in the objective content of each or any of its passing moments. Both the theist and atheist do not expect different events to occur in the successive details of the temporal process. They do not have divergent expectations of the course of history viewed from within. But the theist expects to have the fulfillment of a specific purpose namely that of creating the children of God where as the atheist does not expect when the history is completed.[50]

Levi B. Gresham a Jewish thinker being impressed with the wonder of life and the mystery enveloping it stands as strong evidence to prove the existence of God. His teleological argument establishe. Purposiveness evident in the birth of animals and humans. It is a regular feature of the universe and it cannot be due to chance for chance may produce an occasional perfection but not one so constant and widespread. There is purposiveness in the universe as evidenced by birth, which must be under the influence of Intelligence. This active Intellect necessarily belongs to the Divine Mind.

Has has given the version of the cosmological argument. He holds that since every cause has an effect; it follows that any particular effect is only possible but not necessary. The effect only exists because it is cause and if the cause is absent, the effect too would be absent. Since the effect depends on its cause for its existence, it cannot therefore be said to enjoy necessary existence. It is possible for it to exist or not to exist just as it is possible for its cause either to exist or not to exist. The cause also follows the same pattern. The cause itself is an effect with its own cause this means that all things are only possible and there is existence yet the universe does exist. To have existence to be necessary not merely possible, there must be a causeless cause, which is God.[51]

Joseph Albo claims that his proof is implied in the creation. It is narrative at the beginning of Genesis. The heaven and earth are created but at different times. The entire creation was potential and became actual during the six days of creation. The experience of senses indicates that things constantly pass from potentiality to actuality. But the cause of this change from potentiality to actuality cannot reside in the things themselves for they would become actual without even being potential. So there must be an actualizing cause, which was not merely potential. This abstract cause, causing all things to pass from potentiality to actuality is God.[52]

### Faith and Reason

The word faith signifies both what is believed and the act of believing. The virtue of faith is the habit of belief and the object of that virtue is what is believed. Faith, though based on reason, transcends reason, involving an act of will and aspiration.[53] It may be taken for granted that faith is necessary if man is to achieve his eternal destiny. One could come to living contact with God, only by faith alone. Man is justified by only faith.[54] Faith is an act of the whole personality with strong emotional elements within it. Emotion manifests itself with the involvement of the whole personality in an act of life or spirit. Emotion is not the source of faith. Faith is definite in its direction and concrete in its content and it claims truth and commitment. It is directed towards the unconditional. It appears in a concrete reality that demands and justifies such commitments.[55]

The modern discussion on faith cannot afford to neglect the question whether the concept of faiths object God is logically meaningful and also whether it makes sense to speak of God. It has been pointed out that the latest challenge to religious belief is more serious than the earlier challenges of atheism and agnosticism. While the atheists deny the existence of God, the agnostics are not sure of God's existence. The new challenge at the first instance came from the ranks of the 'Vienna Circle', which has been elaborated by the logical positivists. There has been much discussion around the meaning of religious language by A. J. Ayer in his Language, Truth and Logic.'[56]

The principle of verification has been accepted to defend religious language as cognitive. But it invokes eschatological verification. The relationship of man with God, involved in Judaism, Christianity and Islam, the belief that the soul of man is immortal and the soul of, good person will enjoy the goodness of God forever. It the belief is true, it will be verified by the good man after the death of his body. If the belief is false, this cannot be determined at any time since there is no God or after life, no man will be in a position to put it to the test. But the belief that it is capable of being verified is sufficient to give it meaning.[57]

Belief in God, the reaching out in trust, the personal relationship, the passionate affirmation of that which is true for the individual all these are termed as essentials in the life of truth. One could believe in a being who actually exists. Belief that there is a God must justify itself without reason. Faith must cohere with the rest of knowledge. When the leap of faith is invoked ignoring reason entirely, it is an open invitation to credulity.[58]

The Hebrew Bible deals with faith in terms of passionate concern and commitment and it recognizes the needs of the individual face to face with his God. If stresses that the man as a whole and not his reason alone must be involved in the life of faith'.[59]

Locke when applied to his third category of propositions, faith became decisively important. In his opinion faith applies properly to things above reason. Some maintain that faith is a higher principle than reason and revealed doctrines contrary to reason must also be accepted.

Reason is held to be a natural revelation through which God communicates to mankind that portion of knowledge, which He has within the reach of their natural faculties. On the other hand revelation is natural reason enlarged by a new set of discoveries communicated.

Immediately by God. Locke says that he that takes away reason to make way for revelation puts out the light of both Human reason does not rise too far from its empirical foundation. Locke uses reason to mean the faculty by which men compare and combine the simple ideas derived from senses. His contention that knowledge arises from sensory experience has systematized the usual understanding of reason. He holds that religion cannot include article of belief that contradict the testimony of senses.[60]

Faith is the central act of the personality and it transcends both the drives of the non-rational unconscious and the structures of the rational conscious. It transcends them without destroying them. The ecstatic character of faith does not avoid its rational character although it is not identical with'. In the ecstasy of faith, the awareness of truth and ethical value are present.[61] In true faith the ultimate concern is a concern about the ultimate, which is true.[62]

William Rowe says

> An act of faith is an act of a finite being who is grasped by and turned to the infinite. It is a finite act with all the limitations of a finite act and it is

> an act in which the infinite participates beyond the limitations of a finite act. Faith is certain in so far as the infinite to which it is related is received by a finite being. Faith includes an element of immediate awareness, which gives certainty, and an element of uncertainty. To accept this is courage. In the courageous standing of uncertainty faith shows most visibly its dynamic character.[63]

Faith admits the application of both the natural order and the supernatural order. When faith is applied to a natural order, it may be equated with opinion or belief. At this level it is natural both in character, in origin and it is distinct from a faith that derives from the high level supernatural order. Supernatural faith runs parallel with natural faith but moves in an entirely different plane. Faith is transcendent as it is divine in origin based on the grace of God. His authority rather than on the authority of man. Such a faith is religious in the strict sense of the term. Supernatural faith excludes all doubts for its truth is absolute as the word of God Himself.[64]

Faith could be used in a sense, by which men live, which has no supernatural origin or cause. One may repose his faith in a set of moral doctrines or ideals taught by the great teachers or revered masters for instance like Plato or Confucius. This illustrates non-supernatural type of faith.[65] Kierkegaard forges a link between authentic existence and genuine faith, which is held to be one of the most brilliant efforts in the history of religious thought.[66]

Faith as a supernatural concept has occupied a significant position drawing the prime attention of many thinkers because of the development of religious thought in the western world.

The attainments of truths such as the existence of God or the immortality of the soul are held to be wholly religious and accessible only through faith. Reason is declared to be quite inadequate and impure that it cannot possibly attain such truth. Others have totally rejected religious truths. They exclude faith and the super natural order. They hold that whatever reason is capable of proving is true, and there is no other source of truth. Some thinkers hold that faith, and reason are complementary. In the event of any conflict between these two faith is the higher court of appeal as it transcends reason. [67] St. Augustine attempts to establish a close union existing between faith and reason, St. Thomas Aquinas brings out with considerable precession the relation existing between faith and reason, the transcendence of faith over reason, and the resolution of conflict between these two.

Faith belongs to propositions above reason revealed by God. Locke made human reason the final arbiter even in the case of those doctrines above reason. He maintained that it is only by exercise of reason could man decide whether those doctrines are truly revealed by God. A strong conviction of the mind or an inner light does not suffice to establish a revelation. Locke insisted that common sense must be the guide. He considered Bible as the word of God confirmed by miracles He accepted on faith for these truths above reason.[68]

Locke stated that faith is inferior to real knowledge. Faith is a settled and sure principle of assent and assurance leaving no manner of room for doubt or hesitation. While knowledge gives certainty, faith gives assurance. Faith stands by itself upon its own grounds. It cannot be removed from them and placed on those of knowledge. He made a distinction of assurance of faith from the certainty of knowledge. He placed faith on a lower plane than the knowledge gained by rational enquiry.[69]

The world as a whole on a divine presence and purpose. God sees the situation as a human being looks upon and appropriate response lies in religious trust and obedience.

He carries into a world which exists through the will of a holy, righteous and loving Being who is the creator and sustainer of all that is. Behind the world, there is apprehended to be an omnipotent, personal will, which guarantees men's highest good and blessedness. The believer finds that he is in the presence of this holy will at all times. Man begins to realize that in his dealings with the circumstances of his own life he has to do with a transcendent creator who is the determiner of his destiny and the source of all good. It is supposed to be an apprehension of the divine presence within that believe human experience It is not an inference to establish a general truth but a man's encounter with the divine and a mediated meeting with the living God.[70]

Reason is an inadequate tool for the comprehension of ultimate reality. But it is the only tool at the disposal of the people to distinguish faith from credulity, true religion from superstition and enthusiasm from fanaticism. When a man is stranded in blizzard, he is compelled to move unsurely along a blindly chosen path. If he is wise, he will try as possible and choose the way he has reason to believe that lead him safely to his destination.[71]

Human reason is very much subject to mistake about divine things when it presumes it as dogmatic because of the limitation of its knowledge. When there is clear evidence from ideas and the principles of knowledge, reason is the proper judge. The characteristic of religious interest depends upon the competence of reason in religion. Reason is capable of perceiving truth in religion.

Reason signifies several things. It implies the superior faculty of the mind furnished with its own notions and axioms. Reason also means an organical thing – the faculty managing a system of ideas and propositions furnished by the sciences and arts. Through such a system; the reason regulates and operates. In the second sense reason is called natural reason. The third use of reason is considered as acting organically with the nobler instrument – revelation. Reasons are same in speculations of all kinds. Right reason is fully informed as is necessary to pass sound judgment on the thing in question. Philosophy, which his basis on the material world cannot validly judge the realm of the spiritual and that eternal.[72]

Belief in reason is an exercise of faith. Faith is an act of reason. Relying on reason in things clearly perceived is to trust in God's veracity and goodness. That is an exercise of faith. The principle of reason does not contradict any article of faith. Faith befriends reason. Reason serves religion. So they cannot clash. They are certain and they are the truths of God. One truth does not interfere with the other. What so ever contradicts faith is opposed to reason, as it is a fundamental belief that God is to believed.[73]

Locke brought religion almost entirely under the dominion of human understanding while analyzing faith and reason. Without of the cherished established beliefs, Locke asserts that every individual has to be worthy of the gift of reason and follow the course. He holds that people are born with faculties and powers capable of almost anything. He proclaims that such would carry farther than could easily be imagined. His purpose of analyzing the boundaries of certainty is not to encourage submission to faith but to direct men away from the futile enquiries into the unknowable. Thereby human efforts may prove useful and reap some useful harvest. Locke believes that man's faculty of reason is the gift of God; the Almighty's noblest creation to impugn or to ignore it, is to disparage. His wisdom.[74]

Lowis Jacobs asserted that from the medieval writings it appears that the use of reason to discover the truth about God is admirable on three counts.

(a) To prove by reason that there is God to keep this belief from subsequent doubt.

(b) The use of reason to discover God to have the effect of refining one's conception of God.

(c) Reason is elevated as the result of the quest.[75]

While examining the relation of reason to faith Locke divided propositions into three categories. Any proposition formulated must be in accordance with reason, above reason or contradictory to reason. According to the propositions of reason the truth could be traced from the simple ideas gained through sensation and reflection. But above reason are these propositions, which cannot be derived from simple ideas. Some propositions are contradictory to reason. They are in consistent and irreconcilable to the human clear and distinct ideas.[76]

Kant holds that reason is confined to phenomena. It does not have the knowledge of moumena or things in –themselves. Phenomena are not something given or merely received or revealed. It is constructed by mind out of a given material and the manifold sense impressions.

Scriptures inspired of God is not a part of the philosophical disciplines, discovered by human reason. So besides the Philosophical disciplines there should be another science inspired of God, with regard to those truths about God. Which human reason can investigate, it is necessary that man be taught by a divine revelation. Only a few could know the truth about God through the human reason with many errors and that admixture of errors. So it is necessary to know the truth through the divine revelation. Apart from the philosophical disciplines, investigated by reason, the sacred doctrine by way of revelation will be made known. The things that are beyond the human knowledge may not be sought by man's reason; the revealed things by God have to be accepted by faith alone. [77]

## REFERENCES


1. Frederic Ferre, *Basic Modern Philosophy of Religion*, pp.121-123.
2. *Ibid*, p.124.
3. *Ibid*, pp.125-126.
4. C.H. Dodd, *The Authority of the Bible*, p.111.
5. Paul Tillich, *Systematic Theology*- I, p.237.
6. Robert W. Hall, *Studies in Religious Philosophy*, 355-56.
7. *Ibid*, p.362.
8. *Ibid*, p.363.
9. *Ibid*, p.359.
10. Lowis Jacobs, *Faith*, p.53.
11. *Ibid*, pp. 62-63.
12. A. John Hick, *The Existence of God*, p. 23.
13. *Ibid*, p.1
14. *Ibid*, p.23.
15. *Ibid*, p.25
16. *Ibid*, p.25
17. Baruch, A. Brody, *Readings in the Philosophy in the Religion*, p. 3
18. John Caird, *An Introduction to the Philosophy of Religion*, p.145
19. *Ibid*, p.150.
20. John Hick, *Philosophy of Religion*, pp.15-16
21. Anselm. *Pros Logion*, 2nd Chapter.
22. John Hick, *Philosophy of Religion*, p17
23. *Ibid*, p.17.
24. John Caird, *An Introduction to the Philosophy of Religion*, p.126.
25. *Ibid*, p.127.
26. *Ibid*, p.129.
27. *Ibid*, p.131.

28. *Ibid*, p.131
29. *Ibid*, pp.134 -36.
30. John Hick, *Philosophy of Religion*, p20.
31. A. John Hick, *The Existence of God*, p, 86
32. *Ibid*, p.87.
33. *Ibid*, p.89.
34. *Ibid*, p.90.
35. *Ibid*, p.31.
36. *Ibid*, p.
37. *Ibid*, p33
38. Ninian Smart, *Historical Selections in the Philosophy of Religion*, p.66.
39. *Ibid*, p.67.
40. *Ibid*, p.68.
41. *Ibid*, p.68.
42. *Ibid*, p.69.
43. *Ibid*, p.69
44. *Ibid*, p.70.
45. A. John Hick, *The Existence of God*, pp.33-34.
46. *Ibid*, p.18.
47. *Ibid*, p.18.
48. *Ibid*, p.40.
49. Denial J. Bernstein, *Approaches to the Philosophy of Religion*, p.276.
50. John Hick, *The Existence of God*, p.261.
51. Lowis Jacob, *Faith*, p.57.
52. *Ibid*, pp.57-58.
53. R.C. Mortimer, *The Elements of Moral Theology*, p.114.
54. *Ibid*, p.116.
55. William. I. Rowe, *Philosophy of Religion*, p. 383.
56. Lowis Jacobs, *Faith*, p.19.
57. *Ibid*, p.30.

58. *Ibid*, p.75.
59. *Ibid*, p.79.
60. Richard S. Westfall, *Science and Religion in Seventh Century*, p.187.
61. William. I. Rowe, *Philosophy of Religion*, p.370.
62. *Ibid*, p.372.
63. Richard S. Westfall, *Science and Religion in Seventh Century*, p.375.
64. John. A. Mourant, *Readings in the Philosophy of Religion*, p.230.
65. *Ibid*, p.230.
66. Malcolm, L. Diamond, *Contemporary Philosophy and Religious Thought*, p. 165.
67. John. A. Mourant, *Readings in the Philosophy of Religion*, p.231.
68. Richard S. Westfall, *Science and Religion in Seventh Century*, p.184
69. *Ibid*, p.185.
70. Robert. W. Hall., *Studies in Religious Philosophy*, p. 180.
71. Lowis Jacobs, *Faith*, p.722.
72. Richard S. Westfall, *Science and Religion in Seventh Century*, pp.172-73.
73. *Ibid*, p.179.
74. *Ibid*, pp.182-83.
75. Lowis Jacobs, *Faith*, p.41.
76. Richard S. Westfall, *Science and Religion in Seventh Century*, p.184.
77. Ninian Smart, *Historical Selections in the Philosophy of Religion*, p.62.

# 4

# Religion and Morality

Moral Philosophy is a separate branch and it is autonomous. It cannot be a branch of Physics, psychology or Economics. It has its basis in goodness. Goodness is not to be confused with expediency, utility or such other matters. Sorrows and pains experienced in realization of goodness have their own value.

In modern times some of the hardest problems are moral in nature rather than those of economic or political problems. They cannot be solved except on religious basis. Man cannot accept his neighbors as fellow brothers unless he leads an austere life and becomes humble. Until man knows of himself, his true self and measures himself in accordance with the revelation of the living God, he cannot become humble Man cannot sensibly talk of morality in the absence of religion.

The fundamental postulate of all rational morality and ethical religion is that the ultimate end of human conduct is to promote the true end of the universe.[1] Religious belief is a particular aspect of a man's total belief about the world. On the other hand religious emotion is not any one's specific emotion but a particular aspect of man's emotional attitude towards the universe or to his ultimate source. Religious conduct is good in general when it represents a right attitude of the will towards the ultimate source of Reality.

Morality deals with what is right or good in conduct. It considers the actions of human beings with regard to their rightness or goodness. It is connected with custom or habit. When the conduct of a person is said to be good people may mean that it is serviceable for the end or ideal in view. The term good also is used to signify not something which is a means to an end but it itself is taken as an end. Thus the Summum Bonum the Supreme good is the supreme end, which the people aim at.

Morality is related to conduct and it is stated to be right when it is dictated by reason on moral grounds. The moral reason is purely a formal principle without any connection with any of the feelings or passions of the human nature. But people have their praise for the conduct that springs from feeling rather than from the application of reason.[2]

Religion in India is essentially rational It is free from dogmatism. It attempts to bring about transformation in all the spheres of the human endeavor in the country. The traditionally accepted religious teachings and morals of Mahavira and Buddha gave a new insight and vision to the modern Indian thought.

In Jainism morality is necessary to bring about reformation in human nature. The way to salvation lies in faith in its real existence of knowledge and perfect conduct. Belief in real existence is held to be right faith. The true knowledge without doubt or error is right knowledge. An attitude of neutrality without desire or aversion towards the objects of the external world is called right conduct. Virtue consists in the five-fold conduct of one who has knowledge and faith.

1. Ahimsa. Is stated to be not mere abstention from causing injury but extending positive kindness to all creation.

2. Charity and truth speaking.
3. Honorable conduct such as non-stealing.
4. Chastity to be observed in thought, word and deed.
5. Renunciation of worldly interests and non-possession.[3]

Violence or infliction of suffering is stated to be a great sin. Other sins are untruthful ness, dishonesty, unchastity, covetousness, anger, conceit, deceit, and avarice drag down to the world.

Other sins such as hatred, quarrelsomeness, slander, defamation, abuse of others, lack of self control, hypocrisy and false faith have also been mentioned. The ethical practice of Jainism is more rigorous than that of Buddhism. It looks upon patience as the highest good and pleasure as a source of sin.[4]

Jainism attaches much importance to a person who does not indulge in violence and killing. A person who does not kill and become a cause of killing is considered to be a Brahman. Jainism condemns the exclusiveness and pride born of caste. Jainism is not opposed to casteism and it determines caste by character but not by birth. It is only by one's actions that one becomes a Brahmin or Kshatriya or Vaishya.

> Him I call indeed a Brahman, who finds no fault with other beings, whether feeble or strong, and does not kill nor cause slaughter. Him I call indeed a Brahman who is tolerant with the intolerant, mild with faultfinders and free from passion among the passionate.[5]

Radhakrishnan says that the ethics of Buddhism is based on its psychology. Without correct psychological analysis a sound philosophy and true ethics cannot be obtained. Good acts are those, which lead to the conquest of passions and desires whereas bad acts lead to unpleasant punishments for the evil. Good acts have been done with the motive of happiness in the world hereafter Bad acts are those done with the idea of gaining happiness here.[6]

The Buddha discovered a middle path, which opens the eyes and bestows understanding that leads to peace, insight and to higher wisdom. The eight-fold path namely right belief, right aspiration, right speech, right conduct, right livelihood, right effort, right-mindedness and right rapture represents the morality of Buddhism.[7]

Right belief has got the first place. A man's action reflects what he thinks. Wrong beliefs result from wrong acts. In order to remove wrong views right knowledge is necessary. In the psychology of Buddhism will and intelligence go together., Right aspiration is a product of right vision. It longs for renunciation, the hope to live in love with all. It is the aspiration of true humanity.[8]

Aspiration has to be realized in action. It must find expression in right speech, right action and right living. " To abstain from false hood, to abstain from backbiting, to abstain from harsh language and to abstain from frivolous talk is called right speech."[9]

Right action leads to right living. It is free from lying and deceit, fraud and misleading talk. Right effort consists in practicing control of passions in order to prevent the rise of bad qualities. Right effort cannot be separated from right thinking. The mind that plays and roves has to be controlled to avoid mental unsteadiness. For Buddhism, emotions are failures and disturbances of moral health. Spiritual pride endangers moral progress.[10]

In Buddhism morality is more individual than social. Conduct is broadly distinguished into well-being and ill-being. While the former springs out of unselfishness and springs in the acts of love and compassion, the latter is rooted in egoism and it results in acts of malice, etc.[11] Selfishness is due to man's imperfect understanding and consequent confusion of the bounds of individuality. Unselfishness is due to the right perception of the truth. [12] The higher life cannot be entered in by the undisciplined. Wrong desires cannot be suppressed except by strong will and purpose.[13]

Greek Philosophy marks it's beginning with an enquiry with the essence of the objective world. It is from external nature; the philosophy turns on man himself. The shifting of interest from nature to man leads to the study of human mind, conduct, ethics and religion Socrates has contributed much for the development of the Greek philosophy He has evinced much interest on the problems of man, human knowledge and conduct. He has fought against the challenges that undermine knowledge and threaten the foundations of morality. He found that the prevailing ethical fallacies owe their existence to the prevalence of misconceptions about the meaning and interpretation of truth. His aim is to arouse passion for truth and virtue among the people to acquire right knowledge.

Socrates seeks to find a rational basis for conduct He endeavors to understand the meaning of morality. He discovers a rational principle of right and wrong to evolve a criterion for moral issues. For Socrates knowledge is the highest good., The significance of Socratic ethics contain in his saying " Knowledge is Virtue".[14] Right thinking is held to be the precondition to have right action. In the absence of knowledge man cannot be virtuous. Socrates holds that no man is voluntarily bad or involuntarily good. No person voluntarily pursues evil or that which he thinks to be evil. To prefer evil to good is not the nature of the individual. Man has to examine himself and follow what is truth and right.

For Plato reality is purposeful, well ordered. World as intelligence, guided by reason, directed towards ethical goal.

What ever is good, rational and purposeful in the universe is due to reason. He conceives the universe basically as a rational universe, a spiritual system. Objects of senses; the material phenomena are mere fleeting shadows of eternal and never changing ideas. As the objects are transitory and ephemeral, they have no absolute worth. Only that which endures is real and has value. Reason is the highest good and of absolute worth. Hence the rational part of man is the true part. Man's ideal must be to cultivate his reason. The body is the prison house of the soul. The release from the body is its ultimate destiny. The glory of the world and the lust thereof passes away but reason and truth alone endure. All else is vanity. Matter is imperfection.[15]

It has been thought that some belief in God and immortality are postulated by the moral attitude. These beliefs have bearing on human life. The continuance of human life on earth has a basis for moral effort. It is felt that moral effort is needed to be justified in one's own efforts.

Bradley emphasizes on justification by faith as laid in his *"Ethical Studies"*. The faith to which he refers to is based on the conviction that the realization of good is the purpose of good. That purpose some how may be achieved despite the imperfections that seem to lie in all human efforts toward it. That faith stands it self in some need of justification. The conviction is that the realization of what the people apprehend as good can be made and ought to be made the supreme object of the human endeavors. This appears to be essence of religion. In that context alone it may be maintained that the moral life depends upon a religious conviction.[16]

The knowledge of what is right or wrong is far from the doing of it. An action performed in ignorance cannot be claimed to be morally good. Without religious knowledge, one cannot have a religious life and a religious faith. Knowledge is certainly the condition of all the spiritual experiences with people. It rightly or wrongly helps to distinguish from religion. In the absence of the knowledge of right or wrong, it is not possible to lead a moral life.[17]

Religion is practical in its essence. It is practice, an experience and life. Religion must be necessarily moral. Morality is man's habitual way of evaluating objects, and of seeking them. The relationship that exists between the religion and moral ideal is more direct. It is perhaps more intimate than to the intellectual or aesthetic ideal.

Free will, immortality of the soul and the existence of God constitute the postulates of morality. While ethics deals with the moral ideal, the validity of the moral ideal leads to the question of the ultimate reality. An ideal, which is not rooted in reality, is illusory as it is a mere subjective creation of the human mind. The moral ideal is believed to be the expression of the Supreme Reality. What is ideal in man is stated to be real in God. The moral ideal is eternally realizable in God who is the embodiment of perfection. God maintains and conserves the supreme values. People constantly make efforts to achieve them. So morality is closely bound up with religion.[18]

Moral ideal is infinite and it cannot be realized completely in this finite life. Moral life guarantees the immortality of the soul. Man has infinite capacity for knowledge and for also realizing good in infinite life. So immortality of the soul is necessary to have the infinite moral experience. Existence of God and immortality of the soul are the two fundamental articles of faith found in religion.[19]

Whitehead states that a rational and moral order prevails is identified with God's primordial nature. God is more than the principle of rational selection. He is the final cause, which guarantees the immortality of every actual occasion and the self-realization of the individual.

In the words of Whitehead

> Religion is the vision of something, which stands beyond, believed and within the passing flux of immediate things, something, which is real, and yet waiting to be realized. Something which is a remote possibility, and yet the greatest of present fact's. Something that gives meaning to all that passes and yet eludes apprehension, Something whose possession is the final good and yet is beyond all reach, something, which is the ultimate ideal and the hopeless quest.[20]

Descartes tries to show that by controlling human desires with inner fortitude making themselves independent of the world, they can live really a philosophical life. People must not be diverted from their goal by sensuous longings. The great ideal is spiritual freedom. He considers the intellectual love for God to be ultimately the greatest moral virtue.

While classifying emotions and passions, Descartes explains that passions represent passive state of the soul. He has named six primary passions – wonder, love, hate, desire, joy and sorrow and all other passions are derived from these primary states. The human deliverance occurs when the significance of that which lies in their own power and within their control is realized. The aim of ethics is to give a feeling of independence. He holds that man can never be completely autonomous for he realizes his destiny only by the recognition of the majesty of God.[21]

Moral action according to Aristotle has to be voluntary and consciously a purposive action. The highest good for man is self-realization. A man realizes his true self when he gratifies the supreme part of his being. A virtuous person acts selflessly for his friends and his country. He will be even prepared to die for them. Moral action is fostered by a moral society.[22]

St. Augustine holds that temperance or self-control is love of God. It is opposed to the love of the world. Fortitude is to overcome pain and suffering with love. Justice is stated to be the service of God. Wisdom is the power of right. He holds that faith, hope and charity as interdependent. Without faith it does not profit to the individual and in its absence hope cannot exist. There is no love without hope and no hope in the absence of love. There can be no love or hope in the absence of faith.[22] The highest value in the universe is not to be found in the material aspect of existence but in the spiritual domain. The highest part of man is not his material body or his sensuous impulsive nature but his spirit.[23]

St. Thomas Aquinas holds that God made every thing for the purpose of revealing His goodness in creation. Every creature has to realize the divine idea and reveal the goodness of God by the realization of its true being. The highest good is God. St Thomas holds that the supreme good for man, which he calls blessedness, consists in the realization of his true self. Acts are called moral when they are performed by the rational beings. The action has to conform to the rule of reason, which is the principle of human conduct. The highest knowledge of God is intuitive and the highest good, attainable in the hereafter, endures forever. It yields supreme happiness and it is the supreme goal of human striving. [24]

The immoral character of an external act depends exclusively on the will. An act may be good, but when turned for any immoral purpose becomes bad. An external act such as evil could never be made good by the will directing it to a good end. St Thomas rejects the doctrine that end justifies the means. The appetites of the senses tend to be morally evil. They are so when then fail to conform to the rule of reason.[25]

According to Spinoza the minds highest good is the knowledge of God and the mind's highest virtue is to know

God. Man strives hard for virtue. Virtue, he held is power. Every thing that tends to diminish the power of the body or mind is not good. He describes pity and sorrow as bad and joy as good. Nature demands nothing contrary to nature. It demands that a man loves himself and strives for what ever is useful to him that leads to his greater perfection. He holds that the power of nature is the power of God himself. Each individual has the highest right to have what ever he regards as useful to himself. He says that virtuous action is rational action. Passion is a sign of weakness and slavery. Every man should necessarily seek what is truly useful to him. Nothing is useful to the individual except knowledge.

It is useful to perfect the understanding or reason. Man's highest happiness or blessedness lies in this. Men will be most useful to one another if each seeks his own true good or act under the guidance of reason. Whatever is good for others is equally good for the person concerned. So to love the enemy is good, but to harbor hatred, anger, revenge or contempt is evil. In an organized society justice and injustice, merit and guilt have meaning. Morality is justified on the ground that it makes social life possible. Spinoza's ethics is individualistic in the sense that its fundamental motive is the desire to achieve individual perfection or happiness. He states that the highest good of the mind is to have the knowledge of God. The highest virtue of the mind is to know God.[26]

Locke holds that men compare their actions with the laws or rules in accordance to their agreement or disagreement with them and call them good or evil. The virtue in all its truthfulness is the will of God. The will of God and His law constitute the only ultimate touchstone of morality. The virtues and the vices are everywhere the same. They correspond with the unchangeable rule of right and wrong established by the law of God. The obedience of people to the laws of God advances the general good to them.

Locke recognizes three modes of moral knowledge. There is an empirical knowledge of right and wrong, a demonstrative knowledge and a revealed knowledge. God arranged in such a manner so as to give a desire for happiness in human nature. Man evolves a moral code in order to promote his happiness. God also has endowed man with reason to enable him to acquire moral truth by demonstration. Finally God revealed the same laws in scriptures, which could be reached by human experience and reason.[27]

## Kant's Conception of Religion and Morals

Immanuel Kant states that there is nothing absolutely good in this world except a good will. A will is good when it is determined by respect for the moral law, or the consciousness of duty. An act performed with inclination or out of self-love or sympathy is not moral. It must be performed with sheer respect for the law. Moreover the rightness or wrongness of an act does not depend upon its effects or consequences. Whether an act results in happiness or perfection is immaterial so long as the motive of the agent is good, He holds that the pure respect for the law is the sole motive of genuine morality. The moral law is a categorical imperative. It is unconditional and imperative duty has to be performed for duty sake. Man has to act in such a manner that he could will the maxim or determines the principle of his action to become a universal law and everybody should follow the principle of his action. This law could be stated, as the supreme test of what is right and wrong. [28]

Kant holds that religion must be based on morals. The moral basis of religion must be absolute. Religion must not be derived from questionable sense experience. It must not be corrupted by the admixture of fallible reason. It must be derived from the inner self by direct perception and intuition. There is need to find a universal and necessary ethic followed by a priori principles of morals as absolute and certain as mathematics. Pure reason could be practical has to be established to determine the will independently of anything empirical.[29] He says that moral sense is innate. It is not derived from sense experience. The moral imperative that the people need as the basis of religion must be absolute. Man possesses an innate moral sense that compels him to discriminate right from wrong.

Kant is of the opinion that an action is good not because it has good results or it is wise but because it is done in accordance with the dictates of inner conscience in a spirit of duty. This moral law does not come from the human personal experience.

An individual who is governed by the moral law but not by his impulses, selfish desires; and appetites is free from all these. The brute is the play ball of its wants and instinct. The moral imperative is the expression of man's real self and it is his innermost self that expresses itself in the moral law. The moral law is his command as long as he is a rational being. He imposes the law upon himself.[30]

Kant's conception of morality demands holiness, perfection and an absolutely good will. Man by himself however cannot completely realize this ideal. God alone is holy and perfect. Man has a propensity to sin as he has strong desires. What all he could do is to respect the law to attain a dutiful disposition. The highest good is realizable in the life to come. A character that is perfectly in accord with the moral law is perfectly a moral man. He has infinite worth and deserves all possible happiness. But the moral law does not promise happiness. It is right to do the right whether people are happy or not. Obedience to morality does not guarantee happiness. A moral person will be naturally worthy of happiness. Happiness can never be the motive of moral conduct.[31]

The only thing unqualifiedly good in this world is a good will It is the will to follow the moral law in disregard of profit or loss. One should never mind his happiness but perform his duty. Kant says that " morality is not properly the doctrine of how we may make ourselves happy but how we may make ourselves worthy of happiness."[32] Man has to perfect himself to achieve perfection even if it brings happiness or pain in himself and happiness in others. He has to treat the humanity in his own self or in that of another in every case as an end but never only as a means.

Thomas Hill Green holds that man has ability to conceive of a better state of himself. Man possesses this ability because he is a self-conscious subject It is a reproduction of the eternal self-consciousness. The source of an individual's ideal to have a better state of himself is an absolute ideal existing in the mind of God. The true good is an end. In this the effort of a moral agent could find real satisfaction. His real will and his true self are regarded as unconditional good as something having absolute worth and absolutely desirable. Someone may conceive the realization of the human personality as the highest good whether in the case of an individual or in others to have perfection in the human self and the enfoldment of its capacities. In order to achieve this goal one must, cooperate with others to achieve the same goal. The moral ideal is absolute and common good. What is good for an individual concerned is equally good for others too. Every rational agent shall consider the well-being or perfection of every other agent to be included in his own perfection. Green resolves the conflict between egoism and altruism by defining the moral ideal of self-development to include the fulfillment of others within it.[33]

Green holds that the moral value of an action depends upon the motives or the character, which it reflects. He assumes that a truly moral motive will always produce moral acts. He says that the ultimate form of moral endeavor is a spiritual act in which the human heart is lifted to God in which the entire self aspires to an ideal of personal holiness. This endeavor has an intrinsic value. The good will and the social will could be termed as the spiritual act, which has the intrinsic value. The practical expressions of a good will have an additional value as means. It is because they result in amelioration of human society. The ultimate purpose and justification is to have a holy heart. The supreme value for man is man himself in his perfection. Green seeks to resolve the apparent incompatibility between the ethics or social amelioration and the ethics of saintliness. The purpose of the social reform is to have the perfection of man on the spiritual side and to achieve the development in regard to his character and ideals. Holiness is the lasting mode of this perfection.[34]

According to Bradley the ethical end is not only the realization of the self, but self as a whole. The individual is capable of fulfilling himself by relating his finite ends to ever wider and more inclusive ends, which ultimately are held closely in the infinite absolute Whole. The ultimate end of morality coincides with the ultimate reality, the absolute. The finite self cannot become actually the infinite but could constantly strive to have ever wider and more inclusive ends.[35] This striving constitutes moral progress. Bradley says, "Realize your self as the self conscious member of an infinite whole by realizing that whole is in yourself."[36]

Even if the infinite whole or the Absolute is the ideal to wards, which the human moral endeavors, have been directed, there are intermediate wholes, which fall short of the Absolute. Identification with them promotes the moral development of the individual self. Bradley holds that the intermediate wholes are various communities' institutions and social groups of which the individual is a member. Every individual is a part of many human communities. Family, society and the state are held to gather by force or contract. Every individual finds that he could voluntarily and consciously pursue the ends for himself. Those ends also promote the interests and well – being of the groups to which he is a part. Thereby he could realize it a longer self than the self of his own personal and private interests and promotes the welfare of the communal group. These social wholes to which the self constitutes a part, prescribes norms of conduct for the individual. They embody a system of duties and concomitant rights.[37]

Bradley says

> A man's life with its moral duties is in the main filled up by his station in that system of wholes which the state is, and this partly by its laws and institutions and still more by its spirit, gives him the life which he does live and ought to live.[38]

Moral character of the universe is personified in the form of a righteous and transcendent God. It has been conceived as immanent in the world process itself constitutes as a part of all advanced religious cultures. It has been until recent times a universal belief of civilized humanity in the west. In the modern time the intellectuals believe that values are subjective and relative that the world is not a moral order.[39]

Much of the darkness; perplexity and loss of sanity even the vast increase of neurotic individuals and nervous breakdowns in the modern times, could be traced back ultimately to the loss of faith in the existence of any purpose or plan in the world – process. It has been one of the major results of the work of the mainly devout and pious people who are the founders of modern science.[40]

When morality is placed purely on a secular basis, there is yet a morality, which is true in the case, of all persons and not binding on this or that social group. The secular morality includes, not only the lower range of morality, the minimum of moral behavior required for survival but even the universal love and compassion that have been commanded by the religious vision. The two sources of morality do not conflict and they are joined together and fuse into one.[41]

The moral ideals, the value experiences enclosed in the religious vision are true. From a naturalist stand point, they are merely subjective. But in the eternal order they are eternal truths. The universe contains both frames of reference. They are both subjective and objective. A Naturalist admits the reality only of the time order but the eternal order constitutes a part of the universe. The moral values, which belong to it are in the same sense real and objective. From the standpoint of time, the world is not a moral order but from the standpoint of the eternal; it is a moral order.[42]

Religion is a religion of human experience, which is in contact with reality. Moral values constitute a part of the nature of things.[43] When the perfection in a life without desire and passion is sought' it is to seek the ideal moral life by the destruction or elimination of that to make any moral life possible. Morality is conditioned by the natural tendencies. In the absence of these, it would not be a reality but an abstraction. Morality presupposes relations created by the natural desires and they furnish the material basis. A moral will which has no relation to particular desires is but the blank form of moral life without any positive content or the possibility of acquiring it.[44]

When the essential characteristic of religion is contrasted with morality, it changes aspiration into fruition, anticipation into realization. Instead of leaving man in the interminable pursuit of a vanishing ideal, it makes him the actual partaker of infinite life.[45]

Religion is the surrender of the finite will to the infinite self-denial of all desire; inclination volition that pertain to the individual. It includes the giving up of every aim of activity that points to the individual's pleasure or interest for the absolute identification of individual will to the will of God and oneness of mind and the human will with the Divine mind Individual will is not the future hope and aim of religion.[46]

When all the human impulses, desires-volitions are given up to become the transparent medium and organ of the infinite and absolute will, the life becomes glorified. In this context religion rises above morality. The ideal of morality is ones progressively realized and the religious ideal is realized here and now. In the process of the action which constitutes the beginning of the religious life, self-surrender, faith are involved and the identification of the finite with a life eternal is realized.[47]

When the natural relations existing between morality and religion are examined, the contrast that appears is that while religion is based on the desire for life, morality imposes a rule upon the life of desire.[48] Religion cannot be truly religion until it finds and incorporates the moral life.

In the words of Archibald,

> The principles upon which religion is founded are in the end the only principles capable of assuring to morality the normative standpoint, in the absence of which the distinction of good and evil, of right and wrong, is bound to disappear, upon analysis, in the category of fact.[49]

Though religion and morality are intertwined, they are conceptually distinct. Religion involves beliefs, attitudes and practices that relate human beings to super natural agencies or sacred realities Morality could be understood in human or rational terms. It follows that the use of religious sanctions to support moral conduct is appropriate. The dictates of morality are superior and takes precedence over self oriented considerations. When something is said to be morally not correct, it is a sufficient ground for refraining from doing it. The dictates of morality have considerable authoritativeness and superiority is widely acknowledged.

Confucius says that when a man is not good, he has nothing to do with the ritual. In the Hebrew prophetic tradition purely ritual efforts to please God is one of the hallmarks. The book of Amos gives a classic expression to the theme which states that " I hate I despise your feasts and take no delight in your solemn assemblies. But let Justice roll down like waters and righteousness like an ever – flowing stream.[50]

Religion is not reducible to morality as it is linked with a variety of human interests and concerns. Religious faith finds expression in aesthetic propensities, historical or scientific curiosity speculative and ritual tendencies No one denies the moral concerns in their fullest sense and moral concerns have been a central aspect of religious life.[51]

An individual's religious beliefs express the intimate convictions. Upon this his character and a conduct of life depends. Religious beliefs have an important effect upon the morality of the believer. Whitehead holds that religious belief should be subjected to ethical scrutiny. These beliefs should be examined to see whether their effect upon the direction and purpose of moral character and conduct commands ethical approval.[52] Whether a religious belief commands ethical approval can be tested by making a comparison of the morality it implies with the moral institutions. When a religious belief promotes a moral outlook and a kind of conduct contrary to the civilized moral institutions, there is need to thoroughly examine such belief and modify. Such religious beliefs are not ethically coherent.

If a religious belief is productive of good moral effect, it affirms as a good religious belief. Thereby it be comes as a sanction for right conduct and helps to maintain good social relations. In the words of "conduct is a by product of religion – an inevitable by – product, but not the main point."[53] Whitehead makes a reference to the civilization of human life. He uses the word civilization to a " certain ideal for life on this earth" It " concerns both the individual human being and also societies of men".[54] He regards civilization as an ideal good realizable by men in their moral activity. Man seeks his satisfaction or happiness and the civilized conduct of his morality requires the attainment of an outlook to be connected with the general good to have satisfaction or happiness. The individual interest has to be sacrificed in the interest of the general good. Thus the civilization of society aims at the general good to be a dominant moral interest on the part of its members.

Religion is not something basically theoretical but practical indeed. Attainment of unity, harmony, peace and happiness is the goal of life. Religion gives insight into the way to attain salvation. Man is finite but craves the true infinite knowledge. Man is not a mere finite but there is infinitude in the finitude of man. Biological life tends to decay and wither. Religion is not concerned with facts belonging to the natural world but with values. Apart from the biological and physical needs, he always hankers after some goal, purpose or end of life that might gives a certain amount of coordination; synthesis and harmony to his warring impulses. Man as a moral being lives in accordance to a plan. If he lives without a plan purposelessly and quite passively, he would no longer be a personality.

In the words of Whitehead

> " Religion is the vision of something which stands beyond, behind and with in, the passing flux of immediate things; something which is real and yet waiting to be realized; something which is a remote possibility, and yet the greatest of present facts,

> something that gives meaning to all that passes and yet eludes apprehension; something whose possession is the final good, and yet is beyond all reach; something which is the ultimate ideal and the hopeless quest."[55]

The sphere of morality is marked by the sphere of actions. In the world of imperfection there is much to be done to achieve progress and improvement. Mortality implies duties or commands that have to be executed and they are meaningful in action. Religion is multidimensional. It is social as well as moral. The question of morality arises in society. It is the duty of man to perform his duties towards the members when he lives in a society.

According to Josiah Royce even the sorrows and goodness involved in the pursuit of goodness have their own value. They keep the sense of the ideal alive in human minds. Goodness cannot be interpreted in terms of profit. As it is self sufficient, it is autonomous. In the words of Spinoza "a blessed life is not the reward of goodness but the practice and enjoyment itself.[56]

When the religious basis of morality is perverted into an authority, the protest against religious morality is justified.

The idea of God is itself taken by religious believer to be the idea of perfect goodness. By discharging his duty, and in the cultivation of goodness, the religious believer feels that he obeys God. God without ethical quality will not evoke any reverence awe or love Therefore there has been intimate connection established between morality and religion. There can be no morality cut off from religion.

## REFERENCES

1. Hastings, *The Theory of God and Evil*. p. 281.
2. John S. Mackenzie. *Manual of Ethics*. p. 158.

3. S. Radhakrishnan. *Indian Philosophy*, Vol.1, pp.325 – 326.
4. *Ibid.* p. 326.
5. Max Muller. *The Sarcred Books of the East*. Vol.- X – p. 92.
6. S. Radhakrishnan. *Indian Philosophy*. Vol. – 1. p. 419.
7. *Ibid.* p. 420.
8. *Ibid.* p. 420.
9. *Ibid.* p. 420.
10. *Ibid.* pp. 422-423.
11. *Ibid.* p. 429.
12. *Ibid.* p. 430.
13. *Ibid.* p. 432.
14. Frank Thilly. *A History of Philosophy*. p. 70.
15. *Ibid.* pp. 90- 91.
16. John S. Mackenzie. *Manual of Ethics*. pp. 409-410.
17. Sir. Henry Jones. *A Faith that Enquiries*. p. 14.
18. Jadunath Sinha. *A Manual of Ethics*. p. 33.
19. *Ibid.* p. 33.
20. Whitehead. *Science and the Modern World*. p. 275.
21. Frederick Mayer. *A History of Modern Philosophy*. p. 119.
22. Frank Thilly. *A History of Philosophy*. p. 115.
23. *Ibid.* p. 182 - 183.
24. *Ibid.* p. 233.
25. *Ibid.* p. 234.
26. *Ibid.* pp. 330-331.
27. *Ibid*, pp. 347-348.
28. *Ibid.* p. 442.
29. Immanuel Kant. *Critique of Practical Reason*. p. 31.
30. Frank Thilly. *A History of Philosophy*. p. 444.
31. *Ibid.* p. 445.
32. Immanuel Kant. *Critique of Practical Reason*. p. 227.
33. Frank Thilly. *A History of Philosophy*. p. 561.
34. *Ibid.* p. 562.

35. *Ibid.* p. 567.
36. F. H. Bradley. *Ethical Studies.* p. 80.
37. Frank Thilly. *A History of Philosophy.* p. 567.
38. F. H. Bradley. *Ethical Studies.* p. 174.
39. W. T. Stace. *Religion and the Modern Mind.* p. 49.
40. *Ibid.* p. 102.
41. *Ibid.* p. 263.
42. *Ibid.* p. 281.
43. F. E., *Religion Morals and the Intellect.* p. 173.
44. John, *An Introduction to the Philosophy of Religion.* p.173.
45. *Ibid.* p. 280.
46. *Ibid.* p. 283.
47. *Ibid.* p. 284.
48. Archibald Allan Bowman. *Studies in Philosophy of Religion.* p.75.
49. *Ibid.* p. 99.
50. Holy Bible. *Book of Amos.* Chapter- 5. Verse, 21.
51. Mirca Eliade (ed). *The Encyclopedia of Religion.* p. 105.
52. A. N. Whitehead. *Religion in the Making.* p. 31.
53. A. N. Whitehead. *Science and the Modern World.* p. 274.
54. A. N. Whitehead. *Adventures of Ideas.* p. 352.
55. Whitehead. A. N. *Science and the Modern World.* p. 171.
56. Pringle, A. S. *The Ideal of Immortality.* p.54.

# 5

# The Concept of Evil

The concept of Evil has occupied an important place in human experience. Evil is held to be anything that is unpleasant, repulsive and offensive. Perhaps there is no human being did not wonder why the world should be so filled with grief sorrow, conflict and madness. Evil in its personal roots is not a problem to be solved but a mystery to be explored. Evil is not the problem outside man but a possibility within him. He has to recognize the evil. Evil implies to spoil, to break into pieces and to make worthless. Evil is inclusive of both the evil deed and its consequences. It has within itself the element of decay, decadence, self, destruction etc. But good has the elements of persistence, survival, permanence, value, etc. The values truth, beauty and goodness shall endure. Over the ages man has made attempts to unravel the mystery of evil enveloping the world by means of myth legend and philosophical speculation. There has been no religion in the world without the mention of pain, misery or destruction. The conflict between the existence of evil and the concept of good has plagued philosophers and theologians.

The theologians and philosophers developed three types of evil in the universe. There is natural evil, in the natural world and its fallen state. Secondly there is moral evil. This type of evil owes its existence because of the result of the will of moral being. Finally there is Metaphysical evil that consists of the devil and demons.

The concept of moral and metaphysical evil needs to be separated from the natural to have better understanding. Natural evil refers to events that have been linked to natural disasters such as floods and earthquakes By relying on natural forces or religion, natural religion can be explained. Moral evil refers to the evil things that people do to each other and themselves.

When a person is aware of good, he must also be aware of evil out of necessity. The ancient Chinese philosopher Chu Hsi states that "good and evil have no existence in themselves, but are terms applied to things according to their advantage or injury to oneself or to mankind."[1]

The fundamental aspect of human nature is held to be good but it is evil that corrupts it. The basic goodness of human nature is necessarily connected with the human capacity to choose.

Rousseau says that

> God makes all things good; man meddles with them and they become evil.... wickedness comes from weakness. The child is only naughty because he is weak; make him strong and he will be good; if we could do any thing we should never do wrong.[2]

The scheme of things is essentially good. There is a rational and moral order in reality. Human beings are part of the rational and moral order in their incorrupted state. Evil is due to the human failure to conform to it. The failure is due to the external or internal human failure.[3]

It is only when man develops the inner self, the evil could be brought to light. In the process of realization man begins to unfold his higher self. When man relinquishes his hold on the physical world, he becomes one with the cosmic consciousness thereby harmony and balance result.

Socrates has had immense faith in knowledge. Knowledge is possible if proper method is pursued. Man has to carry out his reasoning properly to gain the right knowledge. For Socrates knowledge is the highest good. He says that "Knowledge is virtue." [4] The absence of knowledge is vice or evil. Socrates calls knowledge virtue and ignorance evil. He holds that nobody deliberately does an evil act knowingly. While committing an evil, a person always thinks that particular act is good in some way. He tries to justify his action.

Plato holds that the Universe is basically rational with a spiritual system. Objects of senses, the material phenomena around are the mere fleeting shadows of eternal and never changing ideas. The objects which are transitory and ephemeral have no absolute worth. Plato states that which alone endures is real and has value. Reason which is conversant with the highest good has absolute worth. So the rational part of man is the true part of man. Man's ideal must be to cultivate his reason. The body and senses are alien to the soul. The body is the prison house of the soul Deliverance from the body is the final goal of the spirit.

The existence of evil is due to the lack of knowledge. Plato believes that if a man could discover what is right, he will never act wickedly. But the problem is to discover what is right or good. How one could arrive at an agreeable opinion about good life when people have difference of opinions.

Plato says that " what destroys as in inequity and solence combined with folly, what says us in justice-temperance combined with wisdom.[5] No person can do evil in his action decreasing the quality and enjoyment of existence. Some human beings may wrongly believe that if they neglect or reject a greater possible good for lesser present good or evil, they will in fact be better off. They might think themselves that there is possibility that this lesser good or evil may not really be so bad.

While explaining the existence of evil, Stoics adopted two solutions to the problem of evil. The negative solution denies the very existence of evil. The world is good and perfect. What is called evil is only relative evil, which is like shadows in a picture or discords in music that contribute to the beauty and perfection of the whole. The positive solution consists in regarding evil, for example disease as the necessary and inevitable consequence of natural processes or as necessary means of realizing the good. The stoics argue that since physical evil cannot affect human character, which alone has intrinsic value, it is not really evil. As far as the moral evil is concerned, it is impossible to have virtue without its opposite virtue grows strong in combating vice. The truth is that the Universe when viewed in cosmic perspective., is a beautiful good and perfect whole in which every part has its own proper place and purpose. No part when considered in relation to the whole is ugly or evil.[6]

St. Augustine holds that God is the cause of every thing. In order to establish His goodness, the evil has to be eliminated. The whole creation is an expression of His goodness. He created the Universe out of His infinite love. So existence of every kind is good and its value has to be judged in relation to the divine will If God has created and predetermined everything and an absolutely good being, he has willed everything for the best interests of his creatures.

Even the so-called evil must also be good in its way. As the shadow in a picture contributes to the beauty of the whole, evil is indispensable to the goodness of the world. Evil is conceived as a defect and as a privation of essence as an omission of the good. All kinds of evil including moral evil have been brought under the concept of privation. God could have eliminated evil altogether from the scheme of things but he used it as a means to serve the good. The glory of the Universe is enhanced by the presence of evil; St. Augustine ascribes a relative status to evil. Evil is necessary to the good. Evil is a privation of the good. It is the responsibility of man to come out the evil. He adopts mutually complementary solution to the problem of evil.[7]

St. Thomas Aquinas regards evil as privation. A thing acts according to its nature, which is good, and it cannot cause evil. Evil is due to defective action on the part of the form or cause or due to the defective state of the matter.

In the case of the moral evil, the defect lies in the will that lacks the direction of the rule of reason and the divine law. When all things are aimed at good, the evil that is realized is out – side their intention. This is stated to be true in the case of the free rational beings.[8]

St. Thomas argues as follows in theiodicy

> The good of the whole is of more account than the good of the part. Therefore, it belongs to prudent governor to overlook a lack of goodness in a part, that there may be an increase of goodness in the whole. Thus the builder hides the foundation of a house under ground, that the whole house may stand firm. Now, if evil were taken away from certain parts of the Universe, the perfection of the Universe would be much diminished, since its beauty results from the ordered unity of good and evil things, seeing that evil arises from the failure of good, and yet certain goods are occasioned from those very evils through the providence of the governor, even as the silent pause gives sweetness to the chant. Therefore, evil should not be excluded from things by the divine providence.[9]

According to Boehm the realization of the importance of evil is the starting point in the world. Man has many wicked drives for lust and power. Human nature at times is dominated by a relentless struggle in which evil frequently triumphs. How evil can be justified when God is regarded as all-powerful and all good. ? Boehm suggested that God is dominated by divisiveness. In God there is plurality. He holds that the wrath of God is the principle of evil. In God both the heaven and hell could be found. The opposition that characterizes the divine nature is applied to nature. Constant struggle and constant opposition could be found. In the words of Boehm, evil has no metaphysical reality. It only serves to heighten the ultimate goodness of the world making the glory of God even more resplendent opposites go together. Light and darkness, goodness and evil, courage and cowardice – they have almost been found together and they cannot be separated – says Boehm.[10]

When asked whether there can be absolute evil, Hobbes answer is definitely ' No'. The so-called absolute good and absolute evils are only the fictions of the human mind. A thing is called good when it is found to be agreeable and a thing is called evil when it is found to be unpleasant. But these concepts should not be imposed upon the metaphysical structure of the universe. His stress is upon the relativity of goodness and evil.

In the words of Hobbes the life of man is " solitary poor, nasty, brutish and short." [11] Hobbes states that when men desire they are said to love and when they tend to hate, they have aversion. In his opinion appetite or desire is good and the object of aversion or hate is evil.[12] Hobbes maintains that moral; philosophy is nothing but the science of what is good and evil.

Hobbes pointed out that

Good and evill are names that signify our Appetites,

> and Aversions; which in different tempers, customs, and doctrines of men, are different: And divers men, differ not only in their judgment, on the senses of what is pleasant, and unpleasant to the tast, smell, hearing, touch, and sight; but also of what is conformable, or disagreeable to Reason, in the actions of common life. Nay, the same man, in divers times, differs from himselfe; and one time praiseth, that is, calleth God, what another time he dispraiseth, and calleth Evil. From whence arise Disputes, controversies, and at last War-And therefore so long a man is in the condition of meer Nature, (Which is a condition of war,) as private Appetite is the measure of Good, and Evill; And consequently all men agree on this, that Peace is Good, and therefore also the way, or means of peace, which (as I have showed before) are justice, Gratitude, Modesty, Equity, Mercy, & the rest of the Laws of Nature, are good: That is to say, Moral virtues; and their contraire Vices, Evill.[13]

Leibniz holds that God is perfect who does not undergo change and development unlike in the case of other monads. God as a monad. He transcends all monads for he is supernatural and super rational, the most perfect and most real being. He is complete and His knowledge is complete. He has created this world according to a plan. His creation is determined by the principle of goodness and moral necessity. But there is evil in this world. God while expressing His nature in finite forms. With limitation and impediment. Such limitations are called metaphysical evils. They result in pain and suffering which leibniz calls physical evils. Sin is a moral evil. Evil is a foil to goodness and beauty. Virtue gains strength to combat evil and evil the spur that to good action.[14]

Leibniz states that evil can be the means to a greater good. In a painting distortion and ugliness could be found.

Yet these may bring out perfection to the greater extent in the work of art. He declares that so called evil gives exercises to the human moral capacities.

Hegel holds that the presence of evil is part of the scheme of reality. What is rational is real and real is rational. The evil must have its place; though the universe is essentially good. It is the evil that makes the meaning of good possible.

Man's attempts to split up reality into essence and appearance, inner and outer, substance and attribute, force and its expression, the infinite and the finite mind and matter God and the world would give false distinctions and arbitrary, abstractions. There is natural necessity in the structure of absolute thought.[15]

Whitehead states that evil primarily stands for disharmony and a lack of proportion. It indicates ethically that the mark is missed. There is definite tragedy in the life of an intelligent intellectual who succumbs to base passions. In the words of Whitehead evil symbolizes the distance between the ideal and the actual.

**Moral Evil**

A Tennant hold that evil is of the moral kind. All things work together as a whole for the highest conceivable good. Partial evil is not held to be evil as it is a condition of universal good. When it is asserted that all things work together for good by all things does not imply each and every simple thing but the sum of things as one whole or complex the universe as a coherent order.[16]

Moral evil does not come out of moral goodness but good comes out of evil and error. Error expresses itself to reveal truth. Evil in its very acquision reveals itself to be the lesser good. It learns by bitter experience that it is the evil.[17]

Moral evil arises out of the sinful inclination of mankind. Several instances of spiritual conflicts with evil power have been recorded in the history.

> Finally, my brethrun, be strong in the Lord, and in the power of his might.
>
> Above all, taking the shied of faith, wherewith ye shall be able to quench all the fiery darts of the wicked.
>
> And take the helmet of salvation, and the sword of the spirit, which is the word of God.[18]

The savoring activity of God is aimed at dealing with evil. Jesus bore suffering and pain on the cross and demonstrated God's love.

> And having spoiled principalities and powers, he made a show of them openly, triumphing over them in it.[19]

Both the physical and moral evil will be eternally banished in the new creation of God.

A person while standing outside of some evil thing may say that thing at yonder looks bad, but God must see it to be good. Man's religion simply means a sort of stoical indifference to the apparent distinction of good and evil. This is infect the practical attitude of even the most earnest man in the presence of evil.[20]

Lowis Jacobs holds that if a man could never cheat or steal there could be no possibility for him to lead a life of honesty and integrity. But earthquakes, diseases, floods and other catastrophes are the evils of the nature. These are the part of the background of struggle against which man finds the good to make it his own. Man is involved in the very idea of the creation of finite world and he strives for perfection because of the existence of evil and imperfection In the absence of evil, there can be no good.[21]

**Human Suffering**

Like prosperity, suffering introduces a test into human

lives. Suffering is inflicted by the material world upon mankind and sentient creatures with the goodness and power of the creator. Pain is essential to some special end and in each single instance suffering may fulfill some particular providential purpose.[22] For religious people suffering comes as a special trial. Evil is also good for some thing. Much of the human suffering, and many of the outrages of this present life upon the human prudence's and the sacred affections seem to be good for nothing. The forthcoming ness of human suffering is inevitably incidental to a moral order.[23] Man himself does not deem his suffering to be an excessive price to pay for the dignity of his ethical status, once he recognizes physical evil to be inevitable in a moral world. [24] The sufferings of this present time are not worthy to be compared with the glory that shall be revealed. Pain is a necessary means or by – product for a moment. Evil has a temporary and necessary place.[25]

Some chosen individuals take upon themselves voluntarily the suffering of the guilty. Suffering involves misery and offers an opportunity to learn something worth while especially patience.

> My brethren, count it all Joy when ye fall into divers temptations;
>
> Knowing this, that the trying of your faith worketh patience.
>
> But, let patience have her perfect work, that ye may be perfect and entire, wanting nothing.[26]

Suffering takes place due to several reasons. When man is alienated from society for sociological or economic reasons suffering arises. In the religious context suffering is a punishment for mans involvement in sin. It is rooted in the divine mystery but profoundly human. It is held to be divinely permitted to have spiritual blessings.

> Where ye greatly rejoice, though now for a season, if need be, ye are in heaviness through manifold temptations:
>
> That the trial of your faith, being much more precious than of Gold that perisheth, though it be tried with fire, might to be found unto praise and honor and glory at the appearing of Jesus Christ.[27]

Suffering and sorrow create sympathy and promotes kindness among men bringing them into fellowship with God's purpose to ever come evil.

Prophets regarded physical evil such as pain, suffering or disaster as something God tolerates in the world though He over rules it and uses it to punish people or nations.

> I form the light, and create darkness:
>
> I make peace, and create evil: I the Lord do all these things.[28]

Instances of suffering are defacto causes or consequences of greater goods. God is capable enough to create the best possible worlds. But all the best possible worlds must contain instances of suffering. They are logically indispensable components. It is for this reason that there are instances of suffering in the world.[29] It follows logically that God has some sufficient reason morally to allow evil.[30] Divine vengeance in the form of pain or sorrow does not imply evil passions in God. Pain may awaken an evil man to reality Till then he will be enclosed in illusion.[31]

The persons have to confront and endure suffering. The suffering is divided into two kinds. One kind of suffering is relatively of simple kind in which persons experience physical pain due to the stimulation of pain nerves. The other kind of suffering is more complex, commonly called 'mental' that plagues the higher reaches and more subtle depths of the human spirit. Both pain and suffering have a psychological component. When the suffering is stated to be mental, it is of spiritual significance, which is ordinarily absent from the physiological disturbance of pain.[32]

Under some conditions, pain even contributes for the growth of qualitative meaning by way of intercommunication. When pain is communicable, it caries with it a meaning of good life. Under some conditions, pain may take on the character of good life.[33] Suffering adds some meaning. It is essentially the meaning but not the present event alone that is the suffering. Suffering even more than happiness leads to a kind of communication where by creativity increases the good life. It is the intermixture of suffering and happiness rather than happiness with suffering is required for this Suffering is intrinsic and essential to the increase of qualitative meaning. Not all suffering under all conditions is held to be good. When it enters as one essential ingredient in creativity only it is good. It is evil when it opposes the creative event.[34] Thus suffering is evil only under some conditions but not in all.

Josiah Royce holds that evil could be classified under two categories namely external and internal. The external seems evil such as death. Pain or weakness of character and the internal evil is will itself. The incidents of death, the unavoidable pains of life, the downfall of cherished plans; the cruelty of fate, are the things to be looked at as opaque. People have to develop an attitude of stoical indifference about them. They are to be treated as the accidents of existence. They have to be experienced as elements an absolutely perfect life. They may have been limited to the use of imperfect means. They are organically joined with the rest of the glorious whole.[35]

Intrinsic good is of two kinds. Opposition to good is also of two kinds. While the evil opposing created good is destructive, the evil opposing creative good is obstructive. Created good could be destroyed. It is always being destroyed in some measure, where as creative good cannot be destroyed. It can be obstructed to some degree. Of these two general kinds of evil, the obstructive evil is the most deadly, even though the word destructive carries a more evil connotation in common usage. People are usually more concerned about the created good rather than the creative. They are more disturbed over the evil that attacks that is in their hands than over the evil that opposes the creation what they cannot visualize. Creative good is held to be the only ultimate and absolute good. So what opposes it is basically more evil than what opposes created good.[36] Evil is capable of destroying the created good but can only obstruct the creative good.

If evil in respect of man is examined, sin, immorality and demonry are found to be the three kinds of evil originated with man. Sin is a resistance to creativity for which man is responsible. Man has to recognize that his responsibility is not limited to instances in which he is consciously aware of obstructing creativity or deliberately intending to do so. Unintended and unconscious resistance is a sinful act. It is because of the consequence of many past decisions for which man is responsible. This does not apply to the mere individual alone but to the society and the race as well. Much resistance in the individual is not intended by him. It is due to the choices made by other human beings. Thus there is a collective responsibility and the individual cannot be held responsible in many cases, as he does not live in isolation. Creativity is essentially and necessarily social.[37]

It is sinful to man to be resistant to the creative event. It is sinful to be rebellious against the will of God. Modern people are also responsible for sin. They are as the people of the past were.[38]

The creature is turned out to be against the creator is another kind of sin – the created good thing turning against the creativity. As far as the personality of man is concerned, it is a created good turning against creativity. Man's personality is a created good. His society, his culture and his ideals are also good. But man refuses to meet the demands for the creative event to rule his life. This is sinful. He holds on to conditions that obstruct the working of creativity.[39]

## Good Will

The moral insight condemns the evil that it experiences. It condemns and conquers the evil with good will. It is only through the inner victory over the evil that is experienced as a conquered tendency, the good will have its being. Since the perfect life of God must absolutely have the good will, it also must be conscious of such a victory.[40]

When a person does a good act, it is an element of God's life. The person concerned directly experiences about the partial moral evil and it could become the universal good. It is relatively a universal good present in him. Overcoming himself, he chooses the universal will. Though the bad impulse is in him, it is defeated.[41]

The evil intent of man which in its separateness would be unmixed evil, his selfish will, his struggle against the moral insight, his evil will of him is no lone some fact in the world but is an element in the organic life of God. In God man's evil impulse forms part of a total good will as the evil impulse of the good man forms an element in his realization of goodness. In God man's separatedness is destroyed and with it his sin as evil. Good will in the infinite is what the good man finds the good will to be in himself namely, the organic total whose truth is the discovery of the evil. God's life is perfect since it includes not only the knowledge of man's finite wicked will but the insight into its truth as a moment in the real universal will.[42]

If a man is good, he would be good by including the evil impulse in a realization of its evil and in an acceptance of the higher insight. If a man is evil, then in himself, as a separate being he is condemned. Just because of man's separation of evil is condemned and therefore is the total life of good that includes man with his condemnation and with the triumph of good over him. Goodness has insight in its very life and it has its elements such as evil impulse and its correction. The evil will may either be conquered in human personal experience and thereby people are good. Human thoughts are corrected as they are related to the whole thought.[43] Goodness as a moral experience is the over coming of experienced evil. In the eternal life of God, the realization of goodness must have the same sort of organic relation to evil as it has with the persons. When a person is truly evil, he is in God just as the evil is in the good man. The person in possession of evil is known only to be condemned and overcome.[44]

Evil seems to be a positive element in the world to make hard the conception of the partial evil as good universally in the aesthetic sense. In it the shapeless parts may coexist with a total beauty of the statue. The fragment of the statue is merely an indifferent bit of stone without character. But evil in this world seems to be in opposition to all goodness. In the moral experience, a wholly different relation of a evil part to good whole could be found. A person's good act is good just because of the evil that exists in it as a conquered element.

Josiah Royce states that by its very reason of its structure it is good. The structure includes the evil will but the whole act is good. It has been said that evil exists as a means to goodness in the world.[45] Tennant holds that the continuous presence of evil is essential to conserve the goodness but the human experience suggests the contrary.[46]

Evil is something actual but not a mere illusion. It would be simply due to defect or shortcoming upon a phase in a process. It is thus something without which the process could not proceed. As the progressive reconciliation of conflicts the remedy of defects and the fulfillment of unfulfilled potencies, the process is one of achievements of good and realization of value. But the realization is not possible without the actual progress of the development. It involves the lower phases. It is the very conflict and strain inherent in the defect of the lower phase that excites the activity of progress. The process of the realization of the good feeds on evil by consuming it in course of correcting it.[47]

Josiah Royce says

> We say that the connection is one of organic part with organic whole; that goodness has its life only in the instant of the discovery and inner overcoming of the evil will, and that therefore any life is good in which the evil will is present only as overcome, and so as lost in the good will. We appeal to the moral experience to illustrate how, when we do good, the evil will is present as a real fact in us, which yet does not make us as a whole bad, but just because it is present as an overcome element, is even for that very reason, necessary to make us good.[48]

The theists declare their belief that God is good. They affirm their faith in the goodness which is inherent in the very structure of things and in a way in which evil is not. While evil belongs to the temporal, good to the eternal. Evil is allowed to exist by Gods decree. It ultimately vanquishes.[49] Goodness in the organism is a struggling element. In the infinite and united thought of God, the unity of goodness is eternally present.

The evil perceived in the universe entirely consists of sin and misery. If sin is due to man's free will; it can not be condemned on the account of its existence. Misery could be explained as the justifiable punishment of sin. On the other hand it would not be possible to justify the existence of misery in the absence of freewill. Then sin must have to be referred to God as its ultimate cause. It would not be possible to regard a being as good to whose nature, the existence of all the evil of the world must be attributed, says John.[50] Freedom which is the greatest good and as a presupposition of real secondary goodness, necessitates the existence of secondary evil.[51]

**Concept of Free Will**

> The problem of evil cannot be ascribed to God at all but due to the independent actions of human beings supposed to have been endowed by God with freedom of the will.[52] In practical attitude, evil is simply what should not be, but does exist. Then the question arises what must be combated. Immense share of suffering results from violence. It is the evil that man inflicts on his fellow being.[53]

God is believed to have created the world not through an emanation of his own being but out of nothing. It implies that the being of the world is fundamentally different from God's being. So evil in the world does not reflect a diminution of God's being but the diminution of a thing's own being brought about by sin.[54]

Augustine holds that free will is a gift of God that enables man to be a moral agent. No righteous action could be performed except by free choice of the will and God for that reason alone. Sin is the abuse of free will and it is the failure to will what is right .It is a rebellious turning away from the goodness of God.[55] God has granted free will to man. He is tested in this world through his deeds and ultimately his will be responsible for his acts.

Kants holds that although individual's natural inclination is for good, there is propensity to evil in human nature.

Kant says,

> Evil is possible only as a determination of free will. and since the will can be appraised as good or evil by means of its maxims, this propensity to evil must consist in the subjective ground of the possibility of the deviation of the maxims from moral law.[56]

Individuals have a propensity to do good but through the exercise of freewill one chooses between good and evil. Evil is held to be due to the independent actions of human beings. For this reason evil cannot be ascribed to God.

In the view of Brightman the evil existing in the world that has no conceivable good purpose is not due to the fact that God wills evil but due to the fact that God finds a non rational content in His nature. Rational and non-rational are the aspects of His unified nature. Though God does not create them, He has to take both into account in every action. God is always morally perfect. He wills consistently the best known but He does not bear with the obstinate disobedient elements of the non-rational. But God is capable of controlling the non-rational element.[57]

Evil may be viewed as a negative element in the process of development. As far as the moral evil is concerned, it is held to be due to the abuse of the freedom of will. Freedom implies the unlimited range of choice either to practice virtue or to commit evils.

One cannot realize the value of good in the absence of evil. The presence of healthy people presupposes the diseased people as well. The presence of evil presupposes the presence of good also. Morality presupposes the freedom of will. Freedom of will has meaning only if there is evil in the world. God permits the presence of evil because it is there. God permits the presence of evil because the human beings are free. In the absence of evil, human beings are not stated to be free. If the human beings are free, their freedom can be understood in their practice of virtue and their free choise to choose between them. When this is admitted to be the real content and meaning of the freedom of will, evil exists necessarily. There may be evil consequences and the performance of actions that are evil in character consequently. If the infinite value and dignity of the individual is not to be bartered for a temporary world, which is of little value, the presence of evil cannot be avoided[58] The reality of the world and the recognition of the freedom of will cannot go together. Though freedom is responsible for evil, it is only through it that goodness or happiness or love or anything worth seeking can be had. Royce holds that evil is real. The existence of evil is part of the God's plan. Ultimately the freedom of will is the final solvent of all the difficulties that afflict the human minds.[59]

Abuse of the human exercise of freedom of will is evil. Wills are given to human beings for the purpose of use but not to abuse.[60]

Descartes holds that moral and intellectual evil could be traced in man's misuse of his endowed faculty of free choice. If man uses rightly the freedom of will God has given him, he could avoid error always.

Descartes says,

> "For what ever I restrict my volition within the bounds of my knowledge-when ever my volition makes no judgment except upon matters clearly and distinctly reported to it by the understanding it cannot happen that I err."[61]

**Classification of Evils**

If an attempt is made to classify the evils, sentient beings are subject to the physical evils. They comprise of all the pains and discomforts which arise from diseases accidents, cold, thirst hunger, burns and so on. Some persons by virtue of an exceptionally healthy constitution, good fortune live from birth to death with their exercise of intelligence in happiness where as others suffer with them.[62] The existence of pain and disease makes possible the existence of sympathy, benevolence heroism. The doctors and the reformers are gradually successful in overcoming these evils.[63]

A second group of evils are those which may be called as psychological evils which include unreciprocated love, separation or death of the beloved, anxiety, fear, frustration and other unhappy psychological states, which cannot be traceable to causes.[64]

Third group of evils are called moral evils. They include all defects of moral character- traits such as malice, hatred, greed jealousy, selfishness cruelty, intemperance and so on which cause suffering to the persons possessed by them or to others. [65]

Lastly there have been intellectual evils such as stupidly, irrationality, insanity, poor judgment, defective perception or ignorance. They prevent a person from dealing effectively with most of the situations he faces.[66]

Evil of any kind, may be intellectual evil, or moral evil, natural or metaphysical evil is always negative and irrational Reality is said to rational and what is rational is said to be real. Some may hold that sin or evil to be rational but human experience does not bear any testimony to such of this kind. Every thing cannot be rational since rationality and irrationality are only relative. Evil and sin are not to be supposed to be rational.

The problem of evil arises out of the relation between the finite and the infinite. As the finite is essentially limited, evil must be its inalienable feature. According to Josiah Royce evil is the most obvious feature of all finite facts.

Josiah Royce says,

> "In the most general sense of the word evil, all finite facts viewed as such, are indeed evil, precisely in so far as when taken in themselves, they have no complete meaning and leave us in disquietude."[67]

When the world is regarded as moral order, the presence of evil cannot be regarded as an unnecessary element in it. On the other hand the presence of evil helps to comprehend the spiritual unity. The existence of evil has a rational justification. In its absence, spiritual strength cannot be obtained. The presence of evil does not stand as a barrier to recognize the reality of the master of life. More over the presence of evils are sources of religious insight.

## REFERENCES

1. Stanford. J. A. *Evil and the Shadow Side of Reality*. p. 7.
2. J.J. *Emile*. p. 5.
3. Kekes. J. *Facing Evil*. p. 125.
4. Frank Thilly. *A History of Philosophy,* p. 70.
5. *Plato Laws* (Trans R. G. Bury). p. 906.
6. Frank Thilly. *A History of Philosophy*. p. 136.
7. *Ibid.* pp.180-181.
8. *Ibid.* p. 236.
9. Baruch A. Brody, *Readings in the Philosophy of Religion*. p. 207.
10. Frederick. Mayer, *A History of Modern Philosophy*.p. 56.
11. Thomas Hobbes, *Leviathan*. p. 65.
12. *Ibid.* p. 24.
13. A. D. Lindsay, *Leviathan*, p. 82-83.
14. Frank Thilly, *A History of Philosophy*. p. 393.
15. *Ibid.* p. 482.
16. Daniel Bronstein, *Approaches to the Philosophy of Religion*. p. 254.

17. Ninian Smart, *Historical Selection in the Philosophy of Religion*. p. 476.
18. *Holy Bible*. Ephesians-6:10, pp.16-17.
19. *Holy Bible*. Colossians. 2:15.
20. Daniel Bronstein. *Approaches to the Philosophy of Religion*. p. 271.
21. Lowis Jacobs, *Faith*. p. 121.
22. Daniel. J. Bronistan, *Approaches to the Philosophy of Religion*. p. 254.
23. *Ibid*. p. 256.
24. *Ibid*. p. 260
25. *Ibid*. p. 265.
26. *Holy Bible*. James. 1:2-4.
27. *Holy Bible*. 1. Peter. 1:6-7
28. *Holy Bible*. Isaiah. 45: 7
29. Baruch A. Brady, *Readings in the Philosophy of Religion*, p. 208.
30. *Ibid*. p. 210.
31. C. S. Lewis. *The Problem of Pain*. p. 83.
32. Henry N. Weiman. *The Sources of Human God*. p. 94.
33. *Ibid*. pp. 94-95.
34. *Ibid*. pp. 96-97.
35. Daniel J. Bronstein. *Approaches to the Philosophy of Religion*. pp. 271-272.
36. Henry N. Weiman. *The Sources of Human God*. p. 86.
37. *Ibid*. p.126.
38. *Ibid*. pp. 126-127.
39. *Ibid*. p. 127.
40. Daniel J. *Approaches to the Philosophy of Religion*. p. 272.
41. *Ibid*. p. 273.
42. *Ibid*. p. 273.
43. *Ibid*. p. 274.
44. *Ibid*. p. 275.

45. Daniel J. *Approaches to the Philosophy of Religion*. p. 276.
46. Ninian Smart. *Historical Selections in the Philosophy of Religion*. p. 478.
47. Errol E. Harris. *Revaluation Through Reason*. p. 116.
48. Daniel J. Bronstein & Harold M. Schulweis. *Approaches to the Philosophy of Religion*. p. 276.
49. Lowis Jacobs. *Faith*. p. 124.
50. Daniel J. Bronstein. *Approaches to the Philosophy of Religion*. p. 318.
51. Wallace I. *The Existence of God*. p. 155.
52. Basil Mitchell. *The Philosophy of Religion*. p. 100.
53. Mircea Elide. *The Encyclopedia of Religion*, p. 207.
54. E.D.L. Miller. *God and Reason*. p. 145.
55. *Ibid.* pp. 146-147.
56. Immanuel Kant. *Religion within the Limits of Reason Alone*. p. 24.
57. Peter Anthony Bertocci. *Introduction to the Philosophy of Religion*. pp. 434-435.
58. Tribhuwan Nath Sharma. *The Religion Philosophy of Royce* pp. 262-263.
59. *Ibid.* p. 271.
60. R.G. Liegge. *Christian Theism in Contemporary Thought*. p. 71.
61. Rene Descartes. *Meditations* (trans). pp. 53 – 54.
62. C.J. Ducasse. A. *Philosophical Scrutiny of Religion*. p. 356.
63. Basil Mitchell. *The Philosophy of Religion*. p. 98.
64. *Ibid.* p. 356.
65. *Ibid.* p. 357.
66. C.J. Ducasse. *A Philosophical Scrutiny of Religion*. p. 357.
67. Josiah Royce. *The World and the Individual*. Vol- II. p. 363.

# 6

# Religion, Society and Culture

The airy things afford no use and satisfaction to the human mind and human society. They are hard to be understood and easy to forget. The conditions prevailing in contemporary society are perilous as they lack the values of life and religion.

The position of modern society is precarious and tragedy is universal. Society has deviated from the age-old traditions, value system and the established law and order. Ideas which were regarded until recently as inseparable from social decency and justice have been swept away. Modern society is rent due to misunderstanding; internal strife's and bitterness. The entire atmosphere is completely disturbed because of suspicion uncertainty and the fear of the future.[1]

Man has to find the necessary remedies for the sick society. Even the civilization in the past has rejoiced in its achievements and progress, but modern society is in anguish, convulsed in agony in the inexorable process of history for its dissolution. Modern man is the recipient of the benefits of science and technology but he is also aware of their bad effects and how catastrophic they can be. Modern man has suffered a fatal shock.[2] The world has to pass through a phase of growing pains as it moves towards a new peaceful world order.

Though there are many races with different languages, customs and traditions, the task before humanity is to create an order in the world and find a way of life by which different groups could coexist peacefully without resorting to force to resolve their differences. The world of today is not intended to be a battleground of warring nations but it is a commonwealth of different groups engaged in the cooperation of constructive effort to achieve human dignity, noble living and prosperity for all.[3]

While some religions and customs are local in character, Science recognizes no boundaries in the socio-political spheres. It speaks a language understandable by all. The impact of science on man is profound that has sheltered the pre-machine world of independent states entirely. The industrial revolution has affected economic relations and humanity has become a world society with a world economy that calls for a world order. Science reveals identical cosmic elements as the basis of human life and philosophy visualizes a Universal consciousness at the back of the nature and humanity but religion refers to the human struggles and spiritual aspirations.[4]

The progress and advancement of the modern world is measured in external and material terms. There is need to regard spiritual values, love of truth – and beauty, righteousness justice and mercy, sympathy with the oppressed and belief in the brotherhood of man. These qualities will save modern civilization, says Radhakrishnan. People should not separate themselves from rest of the world on the ground of religion, race nation or polity. They in no way assist human evolution or progress but retard it.[5]

Civilization is held to be a way of life and a movement of the human spirit. Its essence does not lie in any biological unity of race or in political or economic arrangements but in the values that create and sustain them. In the words of

Radhakrishnan "Every civilization is the expression of a religion for religion signifies faith in absolute values and a way of life to realize them.[6]

In the event of lack of conviction about the absolute values of a civilization its institutions will be in ruins. Religious faith promotes the passion to preserve the way of life. If faith is on decadence, obedience degenerates into habit and habit withers away slowly.[7]

The reign of matter that reigns supreme in the modern world is due to the exclusion of the element of spirit from the human. It is held to be the primary cause. The weakness of modern civilization is because of the defeat of the human by the material.[8] The modern faith is marked by the characteristics of rootless secularism, the worship of man and the state. The opposite spiritual theory that insist that man should live by bread alone cut off the connections of man with the world of spirit and there by integrate him totally with the worldly communities of class race, state and nation.[9]

In modern times people have lost the spiritual consciousness. They suffer from the sickness of the sprit. There is need to find the roots in the eternal and regain the lost faith in the transcendent truth that orders life, disciplines and brings unity and purpose to it. If not, there is no meaning for the human life.[10]

Radhakrishnan says,

> The call of communism to the world has the passion of religion. It challenges existing evils; offers a clear and definite programme of action, and professes to provide a scientific analysis of economic and political situations. In its concern for the poor and the lowly in its demand for a more equitable distribution of wealth and opportunity, in its insistence on racial equality it gives us a social message with which all idealists are in agreement.[11]

Religion is a sort of discipline. It touches the conscience and helps people to struggle with evil sordidness. It saves people from greed, lust and hatred. It releases moral power and gives courage in the enterprise of saving the world.

In ancient time, religion has been mixed up with magic and witchcraft. Unskilled medical practice and superstition. The dogmas were paths to divine life, but today they are hindrances. They should not be allowed to interpose a barrier between man and God, and spiritual life. Religion has to be the binding force. It deepens the solidarity of the human society. Human life and society cannot be changed without the change of human nature.[12]

The human body is a necessary instrument in disguise of the eternal. The truths that are eternal give sovereign rules of conduct for human lives and they are to be realized on earth in social and temporal terms. Religion gives an ethical and social expression. Man is born of some society as a member His life is marked by the network of intimate relations of attraction and repulsions He cannot cut himself free, as it is neither possible nor desirable. In the words of Aristotle a man who is unable to live in society must be either a god or a beast. Moral action is fostered by a moral society.

Modern man can properly evaluate the social and cultural roots of religion as well as the spiritual and ideational aspects of the cultural order with his grasp of the topics of religion and culture functionally.[13] Culture is free to recast its religion. Religion is free to transform the culture in which it operates. Some religions have become, spiritual and ideational foundations of cultures.

From the standpoint of Christian ideology, science has never been permitted to shape the destiny of man. It is because the task of science is merely the instrumental function of seeking facts and discrimination of information about those facts. The influence of science ends there by.[14] Religion is not held to be adequate molder of modern culture. Religion is either obsolete in its solutions to the problems of a rapidly developing culture as John Dewey holds, or it is infantile in its attitudes of wishful thinking and wishful believing in solving the problems of real existence as Sigmund Freud holds. For Karl Marx religion lacks the revolutionary zeal and the power required to bring about the needed cultural transformations. Modern man finds a meaningfull life affecting the vital culture through these three systems.[15]

Religion is the greatest human need. By no means it can be alienated from man. The mystics have become interested in the affairs of the world and in the service of man. Love of god is expressed interms of the human service because service is only an expression of love.[16]

Radhakrishnan says,

> Man's understanding of himself leads to a life of disciplined disinterestedness and of love for all. The brother hood of man is a present possibility. New men with a new instinct to unify, to share, serve and sacrifice are possible. If mankind is released from the pressure of population, if the waste of warfare is avoided, if the sources of wealth are organized by the community, people will become free and adventurous and not lead lives of routine and indolence.[17]

Without showing love to his fellow beings, ritual and belief do not make man religious.

Mohammad states

> Is not that ye shall turn you faces towards the East or the West, but the pious man is he who believes in God and the last day and the angels and gives his wealth for his love of kinsmen, orphans, the poor and the way farer.[18]

Religion produces variable results. The social systems and surroundings of social structures affect the religious systems. Culture is a historically created design for living explicit and implicit, rational, irrational and non-rational that exist at any given time as potential guides for the behaviour of men. Religion is a cultural aspect. Culture must also be seen as social organization. Under many conditions religion as culture could be seen as an integral part of the total culture.[19]

Religious systems enter directly in to the progress of social action and social change. The religious restatements help to redefine the values of society in its contemporary circumstances and help to shape the motives and goals of those individuals who face new opportunities and new threats.[20]

In certain cases religion is accepted by most of the people without thought and conviction but by fear and habit. Many of the aspects of it contradict other conceptions they accept, Religion needs to be examined and thoroughly studied in order to avoid the contradictions. Religion needs to have social relevance and significance. It has to be under stood depending on the human needs, tendencies and potentialities.

Those who identify religion from the supernatural view point of the world weaken religion. Those who regard religion functionally without the belief in specific items of a traditional faith or their inclination towards the natural forces would weaken the religion. The scientific influence may strengthen religion in the long run and renew it in the modern world.

## Scientific Study of Religion

The scientific study reveals the great significance of religion for individuals and groups. It arrives at the conclusion that religion is a permanent, necessary, and inevitable part of human life. The changing content and the basic functions of religion may help to create a situation whereby religion may be adjusted to the contemporary world. More effective in it may more readily develop. By identifying religion with a system of established beliefs and rites, man opposes a developmental approach.[21]

The scientific study of religion explores the interdependence of religion and society. The modern society needs a highly flexible, un -dogmatic religion, that promotes the free study of society in order to find solutions to major moral problems.[22]

All kinds of religion do not fit into the complex framework of contemporary societies equally. While some have upheld faith in religion, others have upheld reason in their constant search for truth to the full extent. For some faith is fixed and final. The scientific analysis tends to arrive at the conclusion that a religious system is necessary for human life. It also suggests that an effective religion must be fully sensitive to human problems, and to the life situation of the contemporary generation.

Mankind has reached a great turning point. Man with his own hand has built the structure of a unified world which are involved by the globalization in economic socio – political, military and communication facts of the modern times. But he has not however developed a cultural system to match the structure and socialization procedures to develop persons who are part of it.[23] Religion in the modern age continues to be powerful age. Religion of the modern times doesnot lack values.

Individual is a part of society. Society is embedded in nurture and nature is the manifestation of the divine. [24] Man has to reflect primarily on his concern for religion and the group.

## Role of Religion in Society

Sociology is defined in terms such as "the study of man in

society" or "the study of human societies" and their cultures. No society is without culture. There cannot be a culture independently of the individuals. Culture is sustained through the human actions. Culture as a system of norms is inferred from the patterned actions of the members of the society.[25]

The integration of society is good. Religion in certain beliefs and practices has become a necessary ingredient of well-integrated society. Religion solves social problems and preserves values. When social patterns change or a religion is transplanted into a new society; the changes that occur indicate the close connection of religion and society.[26]

Most of the cultural patterns, values and the nature of society are intimately connected with religion. The nature of relationship that exists between society and religion depends on the type of society with its size, mobility extent of internal differentiation and other variables.[27] Religion is an essential part of the social machinery. Many persons say that it is true religion that provides the foundation of an orderly social life.

Religion in ancient times was not a system of belief with practical applications. It was a body of fixed traditional practices to which every member of society conformed as a matter of course. Men would not be treated as men if they agree to do certain things without a reason for their action. But in ancient religion, the reason was not first formulated as a doctrine and subsequently became practice. Conversely practice preceded doctrinal theory.[28]

Societies differ in their systems of morals as in other aspects of the social system. What has to be examined in any given society is the established relation of religions of the society to their particular system of morality.[29]

## Religion and Politics

In an undifferentiated society, the institutional role of religion cannot clearly be distinguished from other aspects of the social complex. In pre-industrial societies religion merges with the economic, domestic, political and educational institutions of those societies. The influence of religion permeates the entire fabric of these societies. The laws followed in pre-industrial societies are often of a religious and semi-religious character.[30]

Robert R. Alford holds that the connection between religion and politics arises as a problem in nations that are not religiously homogenous. Classical political thinkers like Aristotle took it for granted that religious homogeneity is a condition to have political stability.[31]

It is held that major pressures against religious and regional politics have been created by social changes because of urbanization and industrialization in countries with secular and universalistic political cultures.[32]

Politics is as essential as religion. Politics if divorced from religion it has no meaning and purpose. Politics constitutes a part of the human being and inseparable from rest of the human life. Man needs to understand political institutions but he also needs a steady light of religious faith appealing to the human heart and intelligence.

Laurence Houseman stated at a reception at Friends House that in Churches all are sinners where as in politics, every one else is a sinner.[33] A man of politics has to be simple and lead an austere life untouched by immorality untruth and political gain.

Mahatma Gandhi stated before group of missionaries that

> "I could not be leading a religious life unless identified myself with the whole of mankind and that I could not do unless I took part in politics. The whole gamut of man's activities today constitutes an indivisible whole……" "I do not know

> of any religion apart from activity. Moral basis to all other activities without which life would be maze of sound fury signifying nothing."[34]

Political power has not to be regarded as an end but as one of the means to enable people to better their condition in every department of life. Politics were to be artificially separated from everything else, from religious values and faith, it would become either a game played accordingly to its own amoral rules that might be a moral disguise if not it would become an illegitimate usurper of religious emotions and needs of the people. Much mischief is being done in the world due to the divorce between public and private conduct.

While making study about religion one has to be more concerned with religious values than beliefs. Dogmas become barriers to religious experience and right knowledge about religion. Politics is always concerned with, "the happiness of the toiling masses, a means to the realization of the highest realizable in life."[35] like religion. Every state is corrupt. It is not possible to fix the boundaries of personal influence in advance especially those who base themselves on eternal truths and become organs of supernatural force. The existing political parties tend to be opportunistic without sticking to any moral principle. People never accept such government that have been founded on force. Modern society is beset with many evils without moral uprightness and no body is inspired to renovate the state on moral and religious principles. As long as the political actions of the state remains untransformed the kingdom of God on earth remains an empty dream.

Mahatma Gandhi states that "politics today encircles us like the coils of a snake from which one cannot get out no matter how one tries."[36] Therefore the only way to wrestle with the snake is to bring religion closer to politics to purify politics. It is not a religion that promotes separatism, violence and fundamentalism needed in modern times, but a religion that upholds human values, international understanding peace and progress keeping politics at the service of humanity is needed.

Politics fundamentally consists of norms. It consists of ways to arrive at decisions, to adopt procedures to carryout certain tasks, human rights and privileges. Politics is concerned with societal norms that stipulate the coercive powers to be used to achieve the goals. Politics balances power relationships and claims.

Religion reinforces its relationship with other societal institutions. Religious norms coincide with political norms. Religion performs an integrating function in society and reduces tensions.

**Religion and Culture**

The problem of the relationship between religion and culture in the modern perspective has to be regarded from the standpoint of the functional approach. Culture could be seen, as a spontaneous consciousness expressed in a peoples mode of existence in their daily life. All the material and spiritual values have been created in the course of history.

The higher value has to be set upon truth than upon any other principle. Human personality sustains because of the culture to which it belongs. Because of the cultural uprooting; structure of the human personality becomes weakened.

Man has to gain the scientific understanding of the reasons. If the human thinking is valid, he can appreciate their ways in the event of need for any change is felt, he can bring about change step by step.

Life of the modern age in a fluid state is rapidly changing. True religion differs from the contemporary culture. There is need to recognize that there is change since the pre-historic times in a gradual accommodation to a world of change and individual action.[37] Religion is a devotion to moral duty. When religious group cultivates ethical values, it is called ethical culture.

The concept of culture has occupied a conspicuous role in the social sciences. Culture is responsible for complex developments in personality growth. Culture is inclusive of the accumulated storehouse of ways of thinking and acting which have arduously been discovered, passed along and added by successive generations. The roots of religion could be traced to heredity and group life. The form it takes is almost entirely a cultural phenomenon. The accumulated wisdom of religious culture is of paramount consequence for the development of religious personality. When culture is unaided, there is no overt religious development of the individual.

Culture is a way of life of the group. The way of life includes the totality of values, norms modes of thinking and the ways of acting shared by the number of people. Culture is the basic setting of the group in which organized activities are grounded.

The social structure of the group includes the concept of culture. The roots of each type of culture are found in social and biological experiences. Culture guides development. The particular pattern, which the personality takes in its religious development, is largely determined by culture. The influence of religion on personality is variable like the patterns of religious experience depending on the belief possessed by human beings.

In the words of P.H. Benson

> "While a comparative study of religious cultures discloses great variability in personality patterns,

> it is the thesis of this text that some patterns of religious culture and personality are superior to others in accomplishing functions of group welfare, personality integration and individual satisfaction."[38]

While dealing with human experience, one must include its relevant aspects; culture tends to be irrelevant in non-human phenomena in the physical and organic area of existence. When the domain of human experience is entered culture becomes relevant. Culture has some of the attractive and elusive qualities. Religion is distinct from its routine, ritual and conventional practices. Religion establishes some sort of relationship with culture.

Karl Marx states that religion cannot be understood apart from the cultural order in which it arises. Niebuhr who seems to be an antagonist of modern culture states that modern man cannot understand his cultural order apart from its spiritual and ideational roots. Culture is held to be inferior to the individual because the self has a radical freedom and a transcendent capacity, which culture does not, posses. Man is next to God whereas culture is next to man.

The issue of the relationship between religion and culture depends upon the conflict-freedom within structure and freedom beyond structure. Religion depends upon the kind of freedom man possesses. The cultural disciplines are not inclined to give man the kind of freedom that enables him to go beyond experience in transcendent acts and thoughts for man does not have the techniques to trace and observe man at the transcendent level. Religious man on the other hand does not have sufficient interest in man. The behavioral sciences admit of some measure of freedom within the structure of man and culture. The meeting ground to have debate is between religion and the behavioral sciences.

Niebuhr claims that Freud, Marx and the modern behavioral sciences obscured the image of man in existence.

There has been a loss of individuality and man's title to freedom in the evaluation of man in the behavioral sciences.[39]

In the contemporary world there is increasing spread of materialism. Religion gives significance to the human fragile and fugitive existence.

Religion has to be capable of responding creatively to fresh challenge to be healthy and progressive. If it fails, it is on the decline. Religions have to be operative and reckon with forces at work and deal with them creatively that they do no fade away.

Radhakrishnan says:

> The spirit of science leads to the refinement of religion. Religion is not magic or withcraft, quackery or superstition. It is not to be confused. With out dated dogmas, incredible superstitions which are hindrances and barriers which spoil the simplicity of spiritual life. Intellectual authority should be treated with respect and not merely inherited authority besides; science requires us to adopt an empirical attitude. Experience is not limited to the data of perception or introspection. It embraces paranormal phenomena and spiritual states. All religions are rooted in experiences.[40]

In the words of Dr. S. Radhakrishnan religion is not a mere intellectual conformity or ceremonial piety. But it is a spiritual adventure. It is based on practice. Final truth cannot easily be found. Religion fulfils human life. Every aspect of human life is raised to its highest extent. Change of consciousness, an inner evolution and change in understanding is needed.

The kingdom of God is the highest state to be attained by man. Truth has to be supported by evidence. For religions human life is an opportunity for self-realization and wrest the immortal from the mortal. It is when mankind comes to know of the truth, universal brotherhood will follow. The scientific temper refines religion.

Religion is not magic quackery or superstition, Religion has not be confused with out dated dogmas, superstitions that stand as barriers, spoiling the simplicity of spiritual life. Scientific temper adopts an empirical attitude. Experience transcends of perception or introspection. All religions are rooted in experience.

The conflict being faced by man is the divine and undivine. Religion aims to overcome the conflict and integrate the personality. Civilizations went on parallel lines, different from one another without an, effect. The inventions made in science and technology, have brought the world into a close neighborhood. This neighborhood one day may be transformed into a true brotherhood. The world must have the feeling of oneness like home in order to save the human race.[42]

Religion is a spiritual change. It is an inward transformation. It is a transition from darkness to light. It breaks the bonds that are laid by the first birth.[43]

## Role of Non-violence

The experiments in international co-operation in education health, science and culture, labour, food, and agriculture an increasing awareness of common interests among the people of the world, the growing consciousness of interdependence among the nations indicate that people are heading towards an international society, a family of mankind.

In the past governments believed in the use of organized warfare. When they were defeated, they did not lose faith in violence. They felt that their defeat is due to inadequacy in military strength and attempted to increase it. A war in the modern time may mean the destruction of civilization. In such a conflict there is no distinction between the victor and the vanquished. The nuclear tests endanger the life and health of the generations to come. The great powers embark on the piling of the armaments and proliferation of nuclear weaponry. Mankind can come out of violence through non-violence. Love overcomes hatred where as hatred results in more hatred.

The Buddha says

> " Never does hatred cease by hating but hatred ceases by love; this is the ancient law."[44]

The exercise of violence leads to the evils of anger and hatred. Non-violence leads to love and truth. Non-violence is life affirming and contributes to human unity progress and peace.

**Human Equality**

Human beings should not be deprived of their dignity on the grounds of their race, color or caste. Man of social conscience is everywhere striving to remove racial discrimination.

Martin Luther King J.R. in USA inspired lakhs of people to fight against the martial Law region in a non-violent manner.[45] Martin Luther King conducted the non-violent resistance movement against the color discrimination in USA. His object was not only to resist apartheid but also to convert rest of his country men the whites into the recognition of dignity and equality of the colored people.[46]

The technique of love and non –violence gave Martin Luther King a potent instrument for social and collective transformation. Blacks could taught this to use in their struggle against oppression and injustice.[47] For Martin Luther King, non-violence is both constructive and its cleansing aspect is the instrument of social progress. When non-violence tends to be constructive, it develops the moral strength of the people and disciplines them for the use of non-violent direct action.[48] While explaining the main characteristics of the non-violent resistance in the Montgomery bus boycott King asserted that his resistance was directed against the forces of evil than against the persons doing evil.

King and the civil rights movements have had an effective technique to force US. President John R. Kennedy and later John son in the right direction. The momentous mass confrontation in Birmingham in 1963 and Selma in 1965 are the outstanding examples of this strategy of action.[49]

## Science and Technology

The technological revolution has spread all over the world. The modern world has witnessed a great improvement in the standards of living. The scientific discoveries have contributed to the comfort of human life. In any fight against disease, poverty, hunger, resources can be used placed at the disposal of science. The living conditions of people can be further improved.

Many people claim that scientific knowledge brings perpetual progress and a steady improvement in human relations. The expected transformation among the people and in their social relationships has not been achieved. However science has liberated man from the tyranny of the environment. But man is not freed from the tyranny of his own nature. The remaking of society depends upon the remaking of the people. Philosophy and religion are as important for human welfare as science and technology.

The authoritarian mind is not consistent with the mind of empiricism of modern science. The scientists maintain that only empirical verifiable evidence has to be treated as true. The assertions about the nature of the universe, of life and death are not same as in science.

Modern science is committed to the mechanistic materialist view. Scientific statements are held to be valid only within the framework of strictly limited relations. The scientist as a part of the universe cannot as a scientist make any statement about the meaning of the universe as whole. Science cannot solve the ultimate mystery enveloping the nature.

For the naturalists the soul of man is nothing but a puff of vapor. The nature of the human self is interpreted in a way that robs of its reality. For the Biologists the individual person is the product of his heredity and environment. According to Psychologists the subconscious mind is the seat of instincts and emotions It is the determing factor in man's life. Sociologists' hold that the social environment in which a man is born mould his mind and character. He is clothed fed and educated as a social animal. His hobbies and amusements are standardized.

Under the influence of the universal experience of religion and modern science and technology mankind is being molded into a single community. There is need for the common man to discover what is uncommon in him and learn to live as a citizen of a world community. Science triumphs over ignorance and superstition and religion over selfishness and fear. Nations will come together to build a great future for humanity and the brother hood of man.[50]

## Place of Man in the Modern Industrialization

Man has become a slave of the machine, which have conquered space and time for him. When spoken in terms of large members and mass organizations the human being is deindividualized. John Ruskin raised his voice against the degrading labour conditions prevailing in the 19th century and the enslavement of man to the machine. Industrialization has reduced the people to the state of slavery. The growth of industrialization has appeared as a menace for the realization of the basic moral ideals of human society.

The author of the book "Future shock, Alvin Toffler lays more stress on the need for the taming of technology.

Alvin Toffler says

> The politics of technology control will trigger bitter conflict in the days to come. But conflict or no, technology must be tamed, if the accelerative thrust is to be brought under control. And the accelerative thrust must be brought under the control if future shock is to be prevented.[51]

There is need to bridge science to the rest of the humanity. Technology looses its purpose if it is not compatible in its working relationships with human values. In the absence of human values, science produces monsters. Technology needs to be within the confines of human values.

Machines to extend to human ability but should not dominate

M.N. Roy says

> Machine should not be the Frankenstein of modern civilization created by man; it must sub serve man's purpose and contribute to his freedom.[52]

The machinery that tends to reduce man into a mere cog in the machine leads to dehumanization.

Bertrand Russell makes out a distinction between the mechanistic out look and the humanistic out look Which stands opposite to the former. Trade union he makes it cleans that if the evil effects of the mechanistic out look are overcome, it would be possible to use machinery for the liberation of life and not for its enslavement.

Russell says,

> The distinction between the mechanistic and the humanistic conceptions of excellence is the most

> fundamental of all distinctions between revial sets of ideals. The mechanistic conception regards the good as some thing outside the individual as something, which is realized through a society as a whole, whether voluntarily co-operating, or not. The humanistic conception on the other hand regards, the good as something existing in the lives of individuals and conceives social co-operation as only valuable in so far as it ministers to the welfare of the several citizens. The mechanistic conception is not interested in individual as such but only in the part that he can play as a cog in the machinery.[53]

Machine has to adjust to man. A balance has to be maintained between the increase in material production and man's spiritual and cultural needs. Man does not exist for science and machines. He has to keep them at the human service to fulfill alone his physical needs but the promotion of higher needs – cultural, fraternal and spiritual.[54]

**Non-violence and Peace**

Sorkin observes

> Through the Universal practice of love hatred, antagonism and injustice would be eliminated and abiding harmony would. Prevail through out the entire human universe.[55]

Violence demigrates the individual. The votary of non-violence enjoys freedom and upholds the human values. Deterrence is a widely understood doctrine for ages. The nuclear deterrence distinguishes it self from earlier practices. Within a short period, two sides can reduce vast areas of the globe to radio active cinders and exterminate hundred of millions of population without sending a single armed soldier beyond the boarders of each side. The doctrine of nuclear deterrence is based entirely on a threat of mutual suicide.[56]

The doctrine of deterrence freezes permanent hostility among nations. The wide range of historical and contemporary human experience enables people to have confidence on non-violence as a human possibility to have political and social security. There are non-violent cultural resources throughout the globe, which can pare the way for the support of disarmament. Non-violence has to be applied in every human aspect of the world situation in order to make the human life meaningful purposive and worthwhile.

Erasmus holds that peace is the order of nature. The celestial bodies move in perfect harmony. Even in the trees and plants there have been signs of unity and love, which are evident. The wild animals and savages do not harm each other. Man, instead of being at war with himself and with his fellow man, could fulfill the supreme obligation of mutual concord and reciprocity of love if he sincerely desires to be so.[57]

## REFERENCES

1. Radhakrishnan, S., *Religion and Society*, p. 10.
2. Jung, C.G., *Modern Man in Search of a Soul*, pp.230-31.
3. Radhakrishnan, S., *Religion and Society*, p.13.
4. *Ibid.* p. 13.
5. *Ibid.* p. 18.
6. *Ibid.* p. 21.
7. *Ibid.* p. 21.
8 *Ibid.* p. 22.
9. *Ibid.* p. 23.
10. *Ibid.* p. 24.
11. *Ibid.* p. 25.
12. *Ibid.* p. 42.
13. J. Clayton Fever & Williams Horosz, *Religion in Philosophical and Cultural Perspective*, p.305.

14. *Ibid.* p.307.
15. *Ibid.* p.309.
16. Tribuvan Nath Sharma, *The Religious Philosophy of Royce's*, p.226.
17. Radhakrishnan, S., *Religion in a Changing World*, p.182.
18. Robert Bellah (ed), *The Concept of Progress in Islamic Law in Religion and Progress in Modern Asia*, pp. 74-7.
19. J. Milton Yinger, *The Scientific Study of Religion*, p. 204.
20. *Ibid.* p. 526.
21. J. Milton Yinger, *The Scientific Study of Religion*, p. 531.
22. *Ibid.* p. 532.
23. *Ibid.* p. 533.
24. Prof. Dwivedi, O.P., *World Religions and the Environment*, p.8.
25. J. Milton Yinger. *Religion society and the Individual*. p. 17.
26. *Ibid.* p. 126.
27. *Ibid.* pp-126-128.
28. J. Clayton Fever, *Religion and Culture and Society*, p.65.
29. *Ibid.* p.75.
30. Eric Carlton, *Patterns of Belief*, p.97.
31. J. Clayton Fever, *Religion and Culture and Society*, p.366.
32. *Ibid.*p.373.
33. Raghavan Iyer, *The Moral and the Political Thought of Mahatma Gandhi*, p. 41.
34. D. G. Tendulakrar, *Mahatma*, pp.387-388.
35. Pyaralal, *Mahatma Gandhi- The Last Phase*, Vol. I., p. 195
36. *Young Indian*, April –1920.
37. Purnel Handy Benson, *Religion in Contemporary Culture*, p.115.
38. *Ibid.* p.489.
39. J. Clayton Fever & Williams Horosz, *Religion in Philosophical and Cultural Perspective*, p.332.
40. Radhakrishnan S. *Religion and Culture*, p.11.

41. *Ibid.* p.11.
42. *Ibid.* p.51.
43. *Ibid.* p.58 .
44. Dr. Vidhya, P.L., *Buddha Brahmapada*, p.53 .
45. Ramjee Singh, *Relevance of Gandhian Thought*, Preface, p.VII.
46. Nirmal Kumar Bose, *Gandhism and Modern Indian*, p.114.
47. Hames Walton, J.R., *The Political Philosophy of Martin Luther King*, JR, p. 43.
48. *Ibid.* p.59.
49. Peter J, Albert, *We shall Overcome*, p.55.
50. Radhakrishnan, S., *Religion and Culture*, p.161.
51. Alvin Toffler, *Future Shock*, p.445.
52. M.N. Roy, *New Humanism – A Manifests*, p.40.
53. Bertrand Russell, *The Prospects of Industrial Civilization*, p.266.
54. J.R. Sethe, *Gandhi Today*, p.101.
55. Pitrim A Sorokin, *Reconstruction of Humanity*, p.46.
56. K. Subrahamanyam (ed), *Nuclear Myths and Realities-Indian's Dilemma*, pp.52-53.
57. Raghavan Iyer, *The Moral and Political Thought of Mahatma Gandhi*, p.219.

# Summary and Conclusion

Religion is a vital force in human society. Although religion is held to be a personal matter; it is a social reality embracing all the values. It is inclusive of the values of Truth, Beauty and goodness. Religion recognizes all the human duties as divine commands. Religion and morality are inseparably bound up with each other. Morality plays a significant role with religion. Radhakrshinan says that the ethical means and the spiritual end cannot be separated. Religion is a life to be lived but not a theory to be accepted. Religion aims at the unity of mankind and a true religious life must express itself in love. The goal of world unity could be achieved by non – violence expressed in Hinduism, Jainism, Buddhism, and Christianity.[1]

Religion is an inward transformation and a spiritual change. It has to overcome the discords within human nature. It is an insight into reality and an experience of reality.

Religion is different from the philosophy of religion. It is an attempt to think critically and comprehensively about religious beliefs. In the philosophy of religion clarity of statements, consistency of claims, adequacy of evidence and validity of argument assume great importance Radhkrishnan stated that philosophy of religion rejects dogmatic method of theology and adopts a scientific view of religious experience. It is a rational assessment of religion.

Humanism has been developed as a substitute for religion in modern times. Radhakrishnan states that "Humanism seems to be religion. The self sufficiency of the natural man, the belief that the only values that matter are human values is the central faith of the hunmanists."[2] It was Radhakrishnan who gave a humanistic interpretation to religion. He says that " Naturalism is right in its insistence on man as body; humanism is right when it exalts man as mind but man is not merely body or mind but it is spirit as well. So humanism can not do duty for an adoring life which is identified with the mind of God, and manifests itself in service."[3]

Radhakrishnan upholds the significance of religion. He further states

> "There is no conflict between religion and a reasonable humanism. The truly religious act in this world; the inner feeling of the relation between God and man is bound to issue in the service of humanity. While what matters is works or fruits of religious life, its social productivity the most efficient servants of society are those who cultivate anxiously the interior life. A religion whose center is man and not God is never a strong one."[4]

Religion binds man to man and man to God. It contributes greatly for the human unity and moral progress. God has to be conceived as reality. He is a necessary being and self-existing. It is impossible to conceive God as non – existing.

The ontological argument for the existence of God was first developed by Anselm one of the most original thinkers who begins Christian concepts of God into the formula " a being then which nothing greater could be conceived" by the word greater he means more perfect rather than specially bigger.

He states that change or the reduction a thing from a state of potentiality to that of action. He holds that a thing cannot be reduced from the state of potentiality to act except under the influence of an agent. Faith is an act of believing. Though faith is based on reason; it transcends reason. Faith is an act and an exercise of reason.

These problems could be solved when humanity takes their recourse in religion 'Know they self' is a popular saying of Socrates. Man has to know of himself and his true self. He cannot sensibly talk of morality in the absence of religion. The fundamental postulate of all rational morality and ethical religion is that the ultimate end of human conduct is to promote true end.

Descartes holds that the intellectual love for God is ultimately the greatest moral virtue. Moral action has to be voluntary. Necessarily it has to be consciously a purposive action. The highest good for man is self-realization. Man becomes virtuous when he acts selflessly. Faith hope, and charity are interdependent. Without faith it does not avail to the individual. In its absence hope cannot exist. There is no love in the absence of hope. There can be no love or hope in the absence of faith.

God made every thing for the purpose of revealing His goodness lies in his creation. The highest knowledge of God is intuitive and the highest good is attainable here after. The character of an external act depends exclusively on will. An evil act could never be made good by the will directing it to a good end. End does not justify the means.

Man necessarily seeks what is truly useful to him. He seeks Knowledge since it is useful to him. The highest virtue is the knowledge about God. In the words of Kant there is nothing absolutely good in this world except good will. A will tends to be good when it is determined by respect for the moral law, or the consciousness of duty. An act performed with inclination or out of self-love or sympathy is not moral. An action has to be performed with respect for the moral law.

Whether an action is right or wrong does not depend upon its effects or consequences but on the motive. Man has to act in such a manner that his will or the principle of his action become a universal law and every body should follow the principle of his action.

Religion must be based on morals and the moral basis of religion must be absolute. Man possesses an innate moral sense and that compels him to discriminate right from the wrong. Man needs to perfect himself. He has to treat humanity in the manner he treats his own self as an end but never as a means to other's ends.

Green holds that moral value of an action depends upon the motives or character. He holds that a truly moral motive will always produce moral acts. A moral ideal is absolute and it is for the common good. What is good for an individual concerned is equally good for others too.

Bradley holds that the ethical end is not only the realization of the self but self as a whole. The ultimate end of morality concedes with the ultimate reality. The finite self cannot assume the position of the infinite but could constantly strive hard to be wider and to be more inclusive of ends. Bradley says, " realize your self as the self conscious member of an infinite whole by realizing that whole is in yourself."[5] Religion cannot be religion unless it incorporates the moral life. Moral concern is a central aspect of religious life.

Whitehead holds that religious belief should be subjected to ethical scrutiny. Whether a religious belief commands ethical approval can be tested by making a comparison of the morality it implies with the moral institutions. When a religious belief promotes a moral out look and a kind of conduct contrary to the civilized moral institutions, there is need to examine such belief and modify, for such religious beliefs can not be ethically coherent.

Religion is multidimensional. It is social as well as moral. The question of morality arises in the society. It is the duty of man to perform his duties towards the members when he lives in a society. In the words of Spinoza. " a blessed life is not the reward of goodness but the practice and enjoyment itself."[6] In the event when the religions basis of morality assumes the perverted position of authority, the protest against the religious morality is justified.

Over the ages man-made attempts to unravel the mystery of evil enveloping the world. Almost all religions have made mention of the evils such as pain, misery or destruction. The conflict that persists between evil and good has baffled the philosophers as well as theologians.

The theologians and philosophers categorise evilness into three types in the universe. There is natural evil in the natural world and its fallen state. Secondly there is moral evil. This is as a result of the will of the moral being. Finally there is metaphysical evil that consists of the devils and demons.

While natural evil refers to the natural calamities and disasters such as floods and earthquakes, moral evil refers to the evil things that people do to each other and themselves. Man is aware of good, he must also be aware of evil done out of necessity. Sin is a moral evil. Evil foils goodness and beauty.

The human nature is held to be good but it is evil that corrupts it. The scheme of things is essentially good. There is a rational and moral order in the universe. Human beings are part of the rational and moral order in their incorrupted state. Evil is due to the human failure to conform to it. When man develops the inner self, the evil could be brought to light. It is in the process of realization that begins in man, he could unfold his self.

Evil has to be eliminated in order to establish goodness. The whole creation is an expression of the goodness of God.

The so-called evil must be good in its way. As the shadow in a picture contributes to the beauty of the whole, evil is indispensable to the goodness of the world. Evil is conceived as a defect and an omission of the good. Evil is a privation of the good. It is the responsibility of man to come out of the evil.

Evil is a means to a greater good says Leibniz. In a distorted painting, ugliness could be found. But this brings out perfection to a greater extent in the work of art. He declares that so called evil gives exercises to the human moral capacities.

In the whole scheme of reality, the presence of evil constitutes a part, says Hegel. The rational is real and real is rational. The evil must have its place though the universe is essentially good. It is the evil that makes the meaning of good possible.

Tennant holds that evil is of the moral kind. All things work together as a whole for the highest conceivable good. Partial evil is not held to be evil as it is a condition of universal good. All things work together for good implies the sum of things as one whole and the universe as a coherent order. Moral evil does not come out of moral goodness but good comes out of evil and error. Man has to develop a sort of stoic indifference to the apparent distinction of good and evil. Earth quakes; diseases, floods and other catastrophes are the evils of nature. Man is involved in the very idea of the creation of finite world. He strives for perfection because of the existence of evil and imperfection. In the absence of evil there can be no good.

Opposition to good is held to be of two kinds. While the evil opposing created good is destructive; the evil opposing creative good is obstructive. Created good could be destroyed but creative good cannot be destroyed. It can be obstructed to some degree. People are usually more concerned about the created good rather than the creative. Creative good is held to be the only ultimate and absolute good. Evil is capable of destroying the created good but can only obstruct the creative good. Creativity is essentially social. The creature turning out to be against the creator is another kind of sin - the created good thing turning against the creativity. As far as the personality of man is concerned, it is a created good turning against creativity. Man's personality is a created good. Man holds on to conditions that obstruct the working of creativity.

Moral insight condemns the evil it experiences and conquers the evil with goodwill. It is only through the inner victory over the evil it is experienced as a conquered tendency, the good will have its existence.

When a person does a good act, it is an element of God's life. The person concerned directly experiences about the partial moral evil and it could become universal good. It is relatively a universal good present in him. By overcoming himself, he chooses the universal will. The bad impulse in him is defeated. Goodness as a moral experience is the over coming of the experienced evil. A person's good act is good just because of the evil that exists in it as a conquered element.

According to Tennant the continuous presence of evil is essential to conserve the goodness but the human experience suggests the contrary. Evil is something actual but not a mere illusion. It is due to defect or shortcoming upon a phase in a process without which process cannot proceed. The process of the realization of the good feeds on evil by consuming it in course of correcting it.

The evil perceived in the universe entirely consists of sin and misery. If sin is due to man's free will it cannot be condemned on the account of its existence. Misery could be explained as the justifiable punishment of sin. On the other hand it would not be possible to justify the existence of misery in the absence of free will. Then sin must have to be referred to God as its ultimate cause and it would not be possible to regard a being as good to whose nature, the existence of all the evil of the world must be attributed, says John. Freedom, which is the greatest good and as a presupposition of real secondary goodness, necessitates the existence of secondary evil.

The problem of evil cannot be ascribed to God at all but due to the independent actions of human beings supposed to have been endowed by God with freedom of the will. Evil is something what it should not be. Suffering arises out of violence and it is the evil that man inflicts on his fellow being Evil in the world does not reflect a diminution of God's being but the diminution of a thing's own being brought about by sin. Sin is the abuse of free will. It is the failure to will what is right. It is a rebellious turning away from the goodness of God. God has granted free will to man.

Kant holds that though individual's natural inclination is for good; there is propensity to do evil in human nature. Through the exercise of free will one chooses between good and evil. Evil is held to be due to the independent actions of human beings. For this reason, evil cannot be ascribed to God.

In the view of Bright man, the evil existing in the world has no conceivable good purpose. God does not will evil but He finds a non-rational content in His nurture. Rational and non-rational contents are the aspects of His unified nature.

Descartes holds that moral and intellectual evil could be traced in man's misuse of his endowed faculty of free choice. If man uses rightly the freedom of will God gave him, he could avoid error always.

The existence of evil is a reality. From the stand point of human experience, it cannot be questioned. Evil is a matter of universal existence. If there were no evil there would have been no religion to counter act evil. Thus the Upanishadic prayer invokes God to lead man from unreal to the real, from darkness to light and from death to immortality.

The presence of evil is a source of insight into reality.

The religion that upholds matter in the modern world is due to the exclusion of the spiritual element from the human. The weakness of the modern civilization is because of the defeat of the human by the material.

People in the modern times have lost their spiritual consciousness. They suffer from the sickness of the spirit. There is need to find their roots in the eternal and regain their lost faith in the transcendent truth that orders life, discipline and brings unity and purpose to it. If not there is no meaning for the human life. Unless human nature is changed, human life and society cannot be changed. Moral action is fostered by a moral society.

The scientific study of religion reveals that religion is a permanent, necessary and inevitable part of human life. It explores the interdependence of religion and society. The modern society needs a highly flexible non-dogmatic religion that promotes a free study of society in order to find solutions to the major moral problems.

In the pre-industrial societies religion merges with the economic, domestic, political and educational institutions of those societies. The influence of religion permeates the entire fabric of these societies. The laws followed in pre-industrial societies are often of a religion and semi-religious character. Religious homogeneity is a condition to have a political stability. Major pressures against religious and regional politics have been created by social changes due to urbanization and industrialization in countries with secular and universalistic political cultures.

Politics is as essential as religion. If politics is divorced from religion, it has no meaning and purpose. Politics constitutes a part of the human being and inseparable from the human life. A man of politics has to be simple and lead an austere life untouched by immorality, untruth and political gain.

It is not a religion that promotes separatism violence and fundamentalism needed in the modern times but a religion that upholds human values, international understanding; peace and progress; keeping politics at the service of humanity is needed. Religion integrates and reduces tensions in the society.

True religion differs from the contemporary culture. There is need to recognize that there has been a change since the prehistoric times in culture. Religions have to be operative in the human life. Religion has to respond creatively to fresh challenges.

According to Dr. S. Radhakrishnan religion is not a mere intellectual conformity or ceremonial piety but a spiritual adventure based on practice. It is a fulfillment of human life. Every aspect of human life is raised to its highest extent. There is need for the change in the human understanding. Truth has to be supported by evidence. For religions the human life is an opportunity for self-realization. The scientific temper refines religion.

The invention made in the field of science and technology have brought the world into a close neighborhood and this may be transformed into a true brotherhood. Feeling of oneness is the need of the day to save the human race. Religion is a spiritual change, an inward transformation and transition form darkness to light.

Modern science is not committed to the mechanistic, materialist view. Scientific statements are held to be valid only within the framework of strictly limited relations. The scientist as a part of the universe cannot make any statement about the meaning of the universe as a whole. Science cannot solve the ultimate mystery enveloping the nature.

In the modern times a balance has to be maintained between the increase in material production and man's spiritual and cultural needs. Man does not exist for science and the machines of the modern world. He has to keep them at the service of man in order to fulfill his physical needs and the promotion of higher needs – cultural, fraternal and spiritual. Religion does not teach to ignore the present life. Religion teaches the humanity to love and serve.

Most of the fundamentalists have very little insight into the fundamentals of religion. People are divided into numerous groups of religion losing sight of the deeper, broader, universal basic elements of religion. They become narrow, exclusive and sectarian in their outlook. Religious system has to be capable of responding creatively to every fresh challenge. Religions have to be sensitive to human ills and social crimes to appeal to the modern man. Religions should not lead to division, discord and disintegration. If religion does not foster unity of understanding and coherence; it falls into the hands of the opponents of religion, says Radhakrishnan.

In future the possibility can be to have only one civilization in the world for it is no more possible for different civilizations to live in ignorance of one another. The scientific discoveries, which have penetrated all parts of the earth, are making the world one though the different civilizations live by and cherish their distinctive principles of life.

Radhakrishnan says:

> The choice before humanity is either cooperation in a spirit of freedom and understanding or conflict

> in an atmosphere of fear, suspicion and jealously. The future of religion and mankind will depend on the choice we make. Concord, not discord will contribute to the establishment of spiritual values in the life of mankind. Concord alone is meritorious said Asoka.[7]

The goal of world unity is to be achieved by ahimsa, (Non-violence) which is insisted on by Hinduism, Buddhism and Jainism. Ahimsa has varied applications, ethical economic and social used by Buddhists and Jainas. People of the world have to be viewed as one family without distinction of caste class or race differentiation by blood descent to achieve the human equality, which is the primary fact. The weapons of war should be turned to the service of peace. The nations form one family and they are inter-responsible and interdependent.

The main causes of the decline of religious belief are traceable to the spirit of skepticism fostered by science, and the exclusive intolerant character of religion. Religion need to get rid of their irrationality, and reactionary character.

Religion is not a way out of life but a way unto life.

In the new society people need a new universal religion. It is not a uniform religion but a religion of awareness, love, wisdom and compassion and truth. Religions must be cured of their provincialism and they have to reveal their universality, without spiritual vagueness or ambiguity.

In the context of the modern world situation Bertrand Russell referred to the Christian virtues – Faith Hope and charity. He asserted that in the modern age the best thing is to cultivate the virtues. Faith. Hope and Charity. This alone helps for the establishment of peace, and harmony among the people. People have to be conscious of the problems confronting them in the modern world and adopt the ideal of unity of mankind as the guiding principle.

Radhakrishnan says:

> The great problems of humanity cannot be solved by general laws but only through the regeneration of attitudes of individuals. Each one should try to over throw the old order within one self. Each one requires to be renewed. Every triumph of human devotion and spiritual energy raises our world to a higher level and brings it nearer the goal of unity of freedom. Man's pilgrimage cannot stop until justice and love sway over the lives of men.[8]

True religion asks us to meet hatred and violence with love.

People must work for a new spiritual reconciliation for they have to meet hatred and violence with love. The recent developments reveal that love is the main aim of living together in harmony.

The present moral; social and political conditions of the world have to be altered before the people have a world community. People have to work out for a world community for the alternatives are chaos or world tyranny.

Jesus' sayings love thy neighbor as thy self, return good for evil and bless those that curse have more relevance and significance than the primitive morality - eye for an eye. There is need to develop love compassion and concern for others. A truly religious man by his life and work sows the seeds of love and tolerance. There is need to foster the root of faith and righteousness without destroying it as Asoka asserted in one of his edicts. People cannot have peace without law based on justice and peace cannot be secured through power.

Man has to understand himself to lead a disciplined life extending love for all. The equality and brother hood is a possibility. If mankind is relieved from the evils that have beset the world and the wastage of warfare is avoided and sources of wealth are properly utilized for their well being they live in peace and happiness in modern world. The search for truth striving for justice and righteousness is essential part of religion in the modern life.

## REFERENCES


1. Dr. S. Radhakrishnan, *Religion and Culture*, p. 34.
2. Dr. S. Radhakrishnan, *An Idealist View of Life*, p. 50.
3. *Ibid.* p. 36.
4. *Ibid.* p. 56.
5. F. H. Bradley, *Ethical Studies*, p. 80.
6. Pringle. A.S, *The Ideals of Immortality*, p. 54.
7. Dr. S. Radhakrishnan, *The Spirit of Religion*, p. 34.
8. Dr. S. Radhakrishnan, *Religion in a Changing World*. p. 32.

# Bibliography


Abel Reuben, *Humanist and Pragmatism*, Prentice-Hall, Inc, Englewood Cliffs, New Jersey, 1975.

Acharayya, K.B *The Modern Philosophical Aspects in Religion*, Varanasi Publishing House, Varanasi, 1984.

Acharayya K.B, *The Philosophical Studies*, Varanasi Publishing House, Varanasi, 1987.

Albert Peter, J, *We Shall Overcome*, Macmillan and Co., Ltd., London, 1940.

Albert Coe. George, *The Psychology of Religion*, The University of Chicago Press, Chicago, 1916.

Allan Bowman Archibald, *Studies in the Philosophy of Religion,* Macmillan and Company Ltd., London, 1938.

Anselm, *Pros logion*, Macmillan and Co., Ltd., London, 1956.

Anthony Bertocci Peter, *Introduction to the Philosophy of Religion*, Prentice - Hall, Inc., USA, 1951.

Atkinson Lee, *Ground Work of the Philosophy of Religion,* The Macmillan Co., Ltd., London, 1976.

Baird D. Robert, *Religion in Modern India*, Manohar Publications, Delhi, 1998.

Baird D. Robert, *Religion in Modern India*, Manohar Publishing, New Delhi, 1981.

Balasubramanian.R., *Perspectives in Philosophy Religion, and Art,* Indian Council of Philosophical Research, New Delhi, 1993.

Bali. Dr., *Introduction to Philosophy*, Sterling Publishers Private Limited, New Delhi, 1989.

Banerjee, B.A., *Religions in India*, Blue Ribbon Book Garden City, New York, 1946.

Basant Kumar Lal, *Contemporary Indian Philosophy*, Delhi, Motilal Banarsidass, 1989.

Battacharayya, K., *Studies in Philosophy in Religion*, Varanasi Publishing Co., Varanasi, 1971.

Bellah Robert (ed), *The Concept of Progress in Islamic Law in Religion and Progress in Modern Asia,* Manoharlal Publication Ltd., Bombay, 159.

Benger. L. Peter., *The Social Reality of Religion*, Faber and Faber Limited, England, 1969.

Benson Purnel, *Handy Religion in Contemporary Culture,* Magnetic Printers Pvt., Ltd, Germany, 1940.

Bertocci Peter Anthony, *Introduction to the Philosophy of Religion,* The Macmillan Co., Ltd., London, 1942.

Bhattacharya. Kalidas, *Studies in Philosophy and Religion,* Varanasi Publishing Company Ltd., Varanasi, 1971.

Blockham, H.J, *Humanism*, Penguin books Ltd., England, 1968.

Bociuriliw, *Religion and Atheism in the USSR and Eastern Europe,* The Macmillan Press Ltd., London, 1975.

Boer, T.J. D.E., *The History of Philosophy in Islam*, Capital Publishing House, New York, 1967.

Boer, T.J. D.E., *The History of Philosophy in Islam*, Gangtous Publishing Company, New York, 1969.

Boer, T.J. D.E., *The History of Philosophy in Islam*, Macmillan Company, New York, 1967.

Boer, T.J. D.E., *The Traditional History of Philosophical Issues,* Mack Muller Co. Ltd., New York, 1967.

Bose, Nirmal Kumar, *Gandhism and Modern India,* Manohar Publishing Co., New Delhi, 1986.

Bouquet AC, *Man and Deity*, W. Heffer & Sons Ltd., London, 1933.

Bradley, F.H, *Ethical Studies*, The Macmillan Press Ltd., London, 1976.

Brody, A. Baruch, *Readings in the Philosophy of Religion,* Prentice - Hall, Inc., Englewood Cliffs, New Jersey, 1974.

Brody Baruch. A, *Readings in the Philosophy in the Religion,* renguin Books Ltd., England, 1969.

Bronstein Daniel. J, *Approaches to the Philosophy of·Religion,* Bankers Printers, Kochin, 1967.

Bronstein.Daniel. & Harold M., Schulweis, *Approaches to the Philosophy of Religion,* Prentice - Hall, Inc, New York, 1954.

Bronstein.Daniel. J, *Approaches to the Philosophy of Religion,* Prentice Hall, Inc., New York, 1954.

Bronstein.Daniel. *Religion, And Moral Activities*, Prentice Hall, Inc., England, 1959.

Caird John, *An Introduction to the Philosophy of Religion*, Glasgow Maclevhose, Jackson & Co., London, 1880.

Caird John, *An Introduction to the Philosophy Religion*, Macmillan Publishing Co., London, 1988.

Carlton Eric, *Patterns of Belief*, Printice Hall., Inc., New York, 1954.

Clayton Feaver J., & William Horosz, *Religion in Philosophical and Cultural Perspective,* Van Nostrand Reinhold Company, New York, 1971.

Clayton Feaver J., *Religion in Philosophical and Cultural Perspective VNR.* Company, New York, 1971.

Clesbseh A William., *Pastoral Care in Historical Perspective,* Prentice Hall, Inc., New Jersey, 1964.

Creuzer & J.D. Guignint, *Studies of Religious History,* George Allen & Unwin Ltd., London, 1952.

Cvade Mircea, *The Encyclopedia of Religion,* Macmillan Publishing co., London,1987.

Dawson. Christopher, *Christianity and the New Age,* Sheed & Warfed, London, 1931.

Descartes, Rene, *Meditations* (trans), Student Christian Movement Press, London, 1932.

Diamond, L. Malcolm, *Contemporary Philosophy and Religious Thought,* McGraw - Hall., Inc., USA, 1974.

Diamond, Malcolm L, *Contemporary Philosophy and Religious Thought,* VNR.Co., New York, 1972.

Dodd Ch, *The Authority of the Bible,* Oildmen Co., Ltd., New Jersey, 1964.

Ducasse, C.J., A *Philosophical Scrutiny of Religion,* the Ronald Press Company, New York, 1953.

Ducasse, CJ, *A Philosophy of Religion,* Christian Press, London, 1954.

Ducasse, CJ, *A Philosophical Scrutiny of Religion,* Macmillan Publishing Co., London, 1989.

Dwivedi, O.P., *World Religions and the Environment,* Manoharlal Press, New Delhi, 1989.

Earnest Hocking. William., *The Meaning of God in Human Experience*, New Haven Yale, Christianity Press, London, 1955.

Edwards B. Rem, *Reason and Religion*, Harcourt Brace Jollamollich Inc., New York., 1972.

Edwards Ram B, *Reason and Religion*, Christian Movement Press, London, 1940.

Eliade Mirca (ed), *The Encyclopedia of Religion*, Macmillan Publishing Co., London, 1989.

Elizabeth. K. Nothingham, *Religion: A Sociological View*, Christian Press, London, 1957.

Emegson Fosdick Harry, *As I See Religion,* Student Christian Movement Press, London, 1932.

Ferre, Frederick, *Basic Modern Philosophy of Religion*, George Allen & Unwin Ltd., London, 1967.

Ferre, Frederick, *Basic Modern Philosophy of Religion*, Henry Holt and Co., New York, 1967.

Fever Clayton, J. *Religion and Culture and Society*, Macmillan and Co., Ltd., London, 1986.

Flew, Antony, *God and Philosophy*, Hutchinson of London, 1968.

Friess Horacel & Herbert W. Schneider, *Religion in Various Cultures*, Henry Holt and Co., New York, 1965.

Galloway D. Phil., DD., George, *The Philosophy of Religion*, T & T Clark, Edinburgh, 1914.

Galloway, George, *The Principles of Religious Development*, Macmillan and Co., Ltd., London, 1909.

Gandhi, Ramachandra, *The Availability of Religious Ideas,* The Macmillan Press Ltd., London, 1976.

Geach Peter, *God and the Soul*, Routledge & Kegan Paul Press, London, 1969.

Geach Peter, *The Virtues*, Cambridge University Press, London, 1977.

George L. Abernethy, *Philosophy of Religion*, Unwin Brothers Ltd., London, 1965.

Glock Y. Charles, *Religion inSociological Perspective*, Wordswarth Publishing Company Inc., California, 1973.

Haffding Harold & B. E. Mayer, *The Philosophy of Religion*, Macmillan and Co., Ltd., London, 1914.

Hagerstrom Axel, *Philosophy and Religion*, Unwin Brothers Ltd., London, 1964.

Hall W Robert, *Studies in Religions Philosophy*, American Book Co., New York, 1969.

Halverson H. William, *A Concise Introduction to Philosophy*, Random House, New York, 1967.

Harris E. Errol, *Revelation Through Reason*, George Allen & Unwin Ltd., London, 1958.

Harry Emerson Fosdick, *As I See Religion*, Macmillan and Co., Ltd., London, 1924.

Heel Gentile Vico, *The Idealistic Concept of Religion*, At the Clare Dom Press, Oxford, 1932.

Henry Jones Sir, *A Faith that Enquires*, Macmillan and Co., Ltd., London, 1922.

Hick, John A, *Existence of God*, The Macmillan Co., New York, 1965.

Hick, John, *Philosophy of Religion*, Prentice Hall, Inc., London, 1963.

Hick, John, *Problems of Religious Pluralism*, The Macmillan Press Ltd., London, 1985.

Hick, John, *The Existence of God*, The Macmillan Co., New York, 1964.

Hick, John, *The Religions of the World*, George Allen & Unwin Ltd., London, 1852.

Hobes Thomas, *Leviathan,* Prentice Hall Inc., New Jersey, 1963.

Holley Raymond, *Religious Education and Religious Understanding,* Henie and Boston, London, 1978.

Holy Bible, - 1 Peter.

Holy Bible, - Colossians.

Holy Bible, - Ephesians.

Holy Bible, - Isaiah.

Hopkins. E. Washburn, *Origin and Evolution of Religion,* New Haven Yale University Press, London, 1924.

Hutchinson, A. John, *Paths of Faith*, McGraw Hill Book Company, New York, 1969.

Hutchinson, A. John, *Ways of Faith*, The Ronald Press Company, New York, 1953.

Huxley, Julian, *New Bottles for New Wines*, The Macmillan Co., London, 1946.

Huxley, Julian, *The Humanist Frame*, Basic Books Inc., New Jersey, 1974.

Huxley, Julian, *The Humanist*, Miftal & Unwin Co., Ltd., London, 1979.

Ishwar C. Harris, *Radhakrishnan. The Profile of A Universalist,* Minerva Associates (Publications Pvt., Ltd.,) Calcutta, 1982.

Iyer, Raghavan, *The Moral and Political Thought of Mahatma Gandhi,* Popular Publishers Co., New Delhi, 1962.

Jacobs, Louis, *Faith,* Basic Books Inc., New York, 1968.

Jevons F.B., *The Idea of God in Early Religions*, Orient Publications, New Delhi, 1978.

John. A. Hutchison & James Alfred Montin, *Ways of Faith,* Orient Publications, New Delhi, 1980.

Jones, Henry Sir, *A Faith the Enquiries*, Basic Books Inc., New York, 1970.

Jung, CJ, *Modern Man in Search of a Soul*, Macmillan Co., London, 1967.

Kant, Immanuel, *Critique of Practical Reason,* Christian Missionary Publications, New Jersey, 1978.

Kant, Immanuel, *Religion Within the Limits of Reason Alone,* Christian Missionary Publications, New Jersey, 1989.

Kekes, J, *Facing Evil,* Avaibility Press, Jerminey, 1970.

Knight, Franks H., *The Economic order and Religion,* Kega an Paul, Trench, Turner & Co., Ltd., London, 1947.

Krishnarao, MV., *Glimpses on Religion, Philosophy and Mysticism,* Sastanga Seva Samithi, Bangalore, 1971.

Kumar Singh. Sachindra, *The Religious Philosophy of Paul Tillich,* Capital Publishing House, New Delhi, 1989.

Lakshman Rao, Ayyagari, *Select Philosophical Papers, Essays and Talks*, A. Chinna Kesava, Rajahmundry, 1980.

Lee Atkinson, *Ground Works of the Philosophy of Religion,* Gerald Duckworth & Co., Ltd., London, 1946.

Legge, R.G., *Christian Theism in Contemporary Thought,* Northember Land Press, London, 1942.

Lewis, CS, *The Problem of Pain,* The Macmillan Co., New York, 1942.

Lindsay, AD, *Leviathan,* J.M. Dent & Sons Ltd., New York, 1962.

MacGregor, Geddes, *Philosophical Issues in Religious Thought,* Houghton Mifflin Company, USA., 1973.

MacIntosh D.E., *Religious Realism*, The Macmillan Company, New York, 1931.

Mackenzie, John S, *Manual of Ethics*, Practical Publishers, New Delhi, 1949.

Mahadevan, TMP. and Saroja. GV., *Contemporary Indian Philosophy*, Sterling Publishers Private Ltd., Bangalore, 1983.

Maritneau James, *Study of Religion*, Oxford at the Clarendon Press, London, 1888.

Marx, K, K. Marx and F. *Engel's on Relig*ion, Foreign Languages Publishing House, Moscow 1955.

Matson I Wallace, *The Existence of God,* Cornell University Press, New York, 1965.

Mayaer, Frederic, *A History of Modern Philosophy*, Classical Publishers & Co., New eland, 1960.

Mehata, PD., *The Heart of Religion*, ornold Heinemann, New Delhi, 1977.

Mehata. J.L., *Philosophy and Religion*, Munishiram Manoharalal Publishers, New Delhi, 1990.

Mensching Gustav, *Structures and Prefers of Religion*, Motilal Banarsi Dass, Delhi, 1976.

Miccer Ed.L., *Theories of Philosophical and Religious Issues*, Dickenson Publishing Company, Inc., California, 1981.

Middleton John, *Gods Rituals*, The Natural History Press, New York, 1967.

Mifcchell Basic, *The Philosophy of Religion*, Jackson Co., London, 1943.

Miller L., Ed. *Philosophical and Religious Issue*, Dickenson Publishing Co., California, 1971.

Miller L. Ed. *God and Reason*, The Macmillan Company, London, 1972.

Miller, *An Idealist View of Life*, Jockson Co., London, 1929.

Milton, Yinger J., *The Scientific Study of Religion*, Macmillan Company, London, 1970.

Misra, R.S., *Studies in Philosophy in Religion*, Bharatiya Vidya Prakasana, Varanasi, 1971.

Mitchell Basil, *The Philosophy of Religion*, Oxford University Press, London, 1971.

Mortimer RC, *The Elements of Moral Theology*, Basil Mitchell Co., Oxford USA, 1989.

Mortimer, DD RC, *The Elements of Moral Theology*, Harper & Brothers, New York, 1947.

Mourant A. John, *Readings in the Philosophy of Religion,* Thomas Y. Cromwell Company, New York, 1956.

Muller Frank, *A History of Philosophy*, Hutchison Co., Ltd., New York, 1989.

Needleman Jacob, A. K. Bierman, Jamesa. Gould, *Religion for a New Generation,* The Macmillan Co., New York, 1973.

Nilleanta Sastri KA., *Development of Religion in South India,* Orient Longmans Ltd, Bombay, 1963.

Nirvendra Nath Swami, *Religion and Modern Doubts*, The Friends Publishing Forum, Calcutta, 1968.

Olson, G. Robert, *A History Introduction to Philosophy,* Harcourt, Brace & World Inc., New York, 1967.

Otto, DD. Rudolf, *The Philosophy of Religion*, Williams and Morgate Ltd., London, 1931.

Parkar, JW., *The Idea of Salvation in the World's Religion*, Macmillan and Company Limited, London, 1935.

Paulsen, Fridrich, *A History of Conceptions of Life and Moral Philosophy*, Oriental Publishers & Distributors, New Delhi, 1978.

Pfleiderer Dr. Otto, *The Philosophy of Religion*, Williams and Norgate, London, 1887.

Plato, Laws, *Trans RG. Bury*, Capital Books Co., California, 1847.

Polland, FE. *Religion Morals and the Intellect*, Macmillan Co., Ltd., London, 1010.

Prem Nath. Ch. S., *The Great Religions of the World*, Crest Publishing House, New Delhi, 1997.

Pyarelal, *Mahatma Gandhi: The Last Phase*, Manoharlal Publishers, New Delhi, 1980.

Radhakrishnan, S, *East and West in Religious,* Allen & Unwin, London, 1933.

Radhakrishnan, S, *Religion and Society*, Clarendon Press, Oxford, 1963.

Radhakrishnan, S, *Religion in a Changing World*, George Allen and Unwin Ltd., New York, 1967.

Radhakrishnan, S, & J.S. Mcirhed, *Contemporary Indian Philosophy*, George Allen & Unwin Ltd., London, 1958.

Radhakrishnan, S, *Bharatiya Sanskruti*, Rajpal & Sons, Delhi, 1974.

Radhakrishnan S, *Indian Philosophy*, G. Allen & Unwin Ltd., London, 1923.

Radhakrishnan, S,*Occasional Speeches and Writings*, Ministry of Information and Broadcasting Govt. of India, Delhi, 1956.

Radhakrishnan, S,*Recovery of Faith*, Orient Paperback, Delhi, 1955.

Radhakrishnan, S, *Religion in Transition*, George Allen & Unwin Ltd., London, 1937.

Radhakrishnan, S, *The Reign of Religion in Contemporary Philosophy,* Macmillan & Co., London, 1920.

Radhakrishnan S, *A Idealistic View of Life*, Black & Son (India), Ltd., New Delhi, 1979.

Ralph Inge KCVO William, *Freedom Love and Truth,* Longmans, Green and Company, London, 1936.

Rama Shankar Srivastava, *Contemporary Indian Philosophy,* Munishiram Manoharlal Pvt., Ltd., New Delhi, 1983.

Rash Dall Hastings, *The Theory of God and Evil,* Tfhe Macmillan Co., London, 1887.

Richard Son Alan, *Science History and Faith,* George Eumberlegece Oxford University Press, London, 1950.

Rousseau JJ, *Emile,* Emberson Press, New Jersey, 1886.

Root H E., *The Natural History of Religion,* Adam & Charles Black, London, 1956.

Rowe William & William J. Wainwright, *Philosophy of Religion,* Harcourt Brace Jovanovich Inc., America, 1973.

Roy, M.N, *New Humanism, A Manifest,* Banish Co., Ltd., California, 1868.

Royce, Josiah, *The World and the Individual,* Macmillan Co., London, 1889.

Russell, Bertrand, *The Prospects of Industrial Civilizations,* Big Men's co., Ltd., New Jersey, 1848.

Santinatha Sadhu, *Critical Examination of the Philosophy of Religion,* Aryabhushan Press, Pune, 1938.

Scott David, *An Exploration in to the Relationship Between Religion Culture*, CISR. And SP. Trust, Bangalore, 1987.

Seshagiri Rao. KC., *Mahatma Gandhi and Comparative Religion,* Motilal Banasidass Publishers Private Ltd., Delhi, 1990.

Seth Pringle A., *Studies in the Philosophy in Religion,* Oxford at the Clariendon Press, Britan, 1930.

Sethy, E.D., *Man in Search of God*, Akansha Publishing House, New Delhi.

Setty, J.R., *Gandhi Today*, Manoharlal Publications, New Delhi, 1949.

Sharan, TN., The *Religious Philosophy of Josiah Royce*, Oriental Publishers & Distributors, New Delhi, 1976.

Sharma, Tribhuwan Nath, *The Religion Philosophy Royce's*, Indian Movements Press, Cuttack, 1946.

Shaw J., *God and The Modern World*, Classical Publishing Co., London, 1972.

Shebbeare J. Charles, *Problems of Providence*, Longmans Green and Co., London, 1929.

Sinclair Upton, The *Profits of Religion*, T. Wermer Laurie Ltd., Briton 1936.

Singh, M. Kirti, *Philosophy and Religion,* Akansha Publishing House, New Delhi.

Singh, M. Kirti, *The Philosophy of Organism: A Comparative Study of Whitehead,* Akansha Publishing House, New Delhi.

Singh, S.K., *Religious Philosophy of Paul Tillich*, Capital Publishing House, Delhi, 1989.

Singh, Ramjee, *Relevance of Gandhian Thought*, Brother Hood Co., Bombay, 1955.

Sinha, Jadunath, *A Manual of Ethics*, Publications House of Delhi, New Delhi, 1967.

Sinha, Raghuyvir, *Religion and Culture of North Eastern India,* Abhinav Publications, New Delhi, 1977.

Smart Ninian, *Historical Selections in the Philosophy of Religion*, Harper & Row, Publishers, New York, 1962.

Solomon, Abraham, *Religion in History*, The Macmillan Company of India Ltd., Bombay, 1972.

Sorokin, Pitrim A. *Reconstruction of Humanity*, The Macmillan Co., Ltd., London, 1889.

Stace WT, *Religion and the Modern Mind*, Christian Publishers, New Mexico, 1842.

Stanford JA, *Evil and the Shadow Side of Reality*, The Macmillan Co., London, 1842.

Subrahamanyan (ed), *Nuclear Myths and Realities — Indian Dilemma*, Publishers & Publishers (India), New Delhi, 1949.

Swinburne Richard, *The Existence of God*, Oxford at the Clavendon Press, USA., 1979.

Temple, William, *Nature, Man and God*, Macmillan Co., Ltd., London, 1953.

Tendulkar, D.G., *Mahatma*, Mehata Publishing Co., Bombay, 1890.

Terril Rasmussem Albert, *Christian Social Ethics*, Prentice-Hall Inc., USA., 1956.

Thomas and Henry, *Living Biographic of Religious Leaders*, Blue Ribbon Books Garden City, New York, 1946.

Thompson, JR. F. Kenneth, *Whitehead's Philosophy of Religion*, Mouton, Parris, 1971.

Tillich, Paul, *Systematic Theology*, The Macmillan Co., London, 1842.

Tillich, Paul, *The Religious Philosophy of Paul Tillich*, Sangita Composing Agency, New Delhi, 1989.

Tiwari KN., *World Religion and Gandhi*, Classical Publishing Company, New Delhi, 1988.

Toffler Alvin, *Future Shock*, Big Men's Publishers, New Jersey, 1942.

Vaxler Adrian, *God Man and Religion*, Ashwin J. Shah, Bombay, 1995.

Verma, KMP, *Philosophy of Religion*, Classical Publishing Co., New Delhi, 1982.

Verma, KMP, *A Critical Philosophy of Religion*, Classical Publishing Company, New Delhi, 1986.

Vidhya, P.L. *Buddha Brahma Pada*, Kolakottam Publishers, Karnataka, 1897.

Vidyarthi, PB., *Early Indian Religious Thought*, Oriental Publishers & Distributors, New Delhi, 1976.

Walten Hanes, J.R. *The Political Philosophy of Martin Luther King Jr.* The Oriental Publications Ltd., Calcutta, 1959.

Washburn Hopkins E., *Origin and Evolution of Religion*, Bharatiya Vidya Prakashan, Delhi, 1942.

Webb, C.J. Clement, *The Historical Element in Rel*igion, George Allen & Unwin Ltd., London, 1935.

Weiman Henery N, *The Sources of Human* God, The Macmillan Co., London, 1920.

West Fall S. Richard, Science *and Religions in Seventeenth Century England*, Yale University Press, America, 1958.

—1920. Westfall Richard S, *Science and Religion in Seventh Century*, Fosdick Publishers Co., Lttd., USA,

Whitehead A.N, *Religion in the Making*, The Macmillan Co., London, 1842.

Whitehead AN, *Adventures of Ideas*, The Macmillan Co., Ltd., London, 1846.

Whitehead AN, *Science and the Modern World*, Basic Foundation Publishers, Bombay, 1916.

Widgery G. Alban, *What is Religion*, Harper & Brothers Publishers, New York, 1953.

Wired, John, *An Introduction to the Philosophy of Religion,* The Macmillan Co., Ltd., London, 1976.

Yarnold GD., The *Spiritual Crisis of the Scientific Age*, George Allen & Unwin Ltd., London, 1959.

Yinger Milton J, *Religion Society and the Individual*, British Publishers, Mexico, 1842.

Yinger Milton J, *The Scientific Study of Religion*, The Macmillan Co., Ltd., London, 1842.

*Young Indian*, April – 1920.

# Index


A

Absolute, 76
Agnoticism, 29
Ahimsa, 64
Albo, Joseph, 52
Alford, Robert R., 116
Angushine, St., 56, 88
Animism, 16
Anselm, St., 39-41
Aquinas, Thomas, 4, 45, 71, 89
  conception of the existence of God, 44
Archibald, 79
Aristotle, 3, 35, 70
Arnold, Matthew, 14
Atheism, 3
Ayer, A. J., 53

B

Benson, PH, 119
Boehm, 90
Bradley, 68, 77, 76
Brightman, 22
Buddha, Gautam, 29, 66, 123
Buddhism, 65, 66

C

Christian ideology, 111
Christianity, 35, 131
Chu Hsi, 80
Civilization, 109
Confucius, 80
Culture, 6, 7, 118, 119

D

Descartes Rene, 4, 49, 70, 103, 133
  on existence of God, 49
Divine Mind, 51
Durkheim, Emile, 18

E

Emotion, 52
Erasmus, 128
Eucken, Rudolph, 15
Evil, 99
  clasification of, 103
  concept of, 85-107
  moral, 92

F

Faith, 54, 55, 56
  and reason, 52
Fever, Clayton, 22
Findlay, JN, 39
Frazer, James George, 19
Free will,
  concept, 101
Fromm, Eric, 28

G

Gandhi, Mahatma, 116, 117
God, 1, 2, 3, 7, 12, 18, 20, 25, 27, 30, 34, 39, 63, 120, 121
 exitence of, 36
  in five way, 47
 Judaic conception of, 35
 proofs for existence of, 34-61
Good will, 98
Green, Thomas Hill, 75
Gresham, Levi B., 51

H

Hayden, Prof., 15
Hebrew *Bible*, 53
Hegel, 14
Hinduism, 142
Hobbes, 90
Houseman, Laurence, 116
Human equality, 123
Human suffering, 93
Humanism, 26, 27
Huxley, Julian, 27

J

Jainism, 64, 65
Jocobs, Lowis, 58, 93
Judiasm, 36

K

Kant, 138
Kant, Immanuel, 2, 4, 15, 14, 25, 50, 51, 59, 74
 on religion and morals, 73
Kennedy, John F., 124

L

Leibniz, 91
Locke, 54, 56, 72, 73

M

Martin Luther King Jr., 123
Marx, Karl, 4, 120
Max Muller, 15, 16
Mill, John Stuart, 15
Modern industrialization, place of man in, 125
Mohammad, 112
Monotheism, 36
Moral philosophy, 63
Moral rule, 17
Morality, 40, 45, 64
Niebuhr, 120
Non-violence,
 and peace, 127
 role of, 122

O

Obedience, 74
*Old Testament*, 35
Ontological argument, 40
*Oxford Dictionary*, 10

P

Philo, 38
Plato, 67, 87
Politics, 116, 118, 140
Present study (the)
 introduction, 1-8
 summary and conclusion, 131-144

R

Radhakrishnan, S., 3, 20, 21, 26, 65, 109, 110, 112, 121, 131, 132, 141, 140, 143
Reason, 54, 57, 58, 59
Religion, 1, 6, 69, 78, 79
 and agnoticism, 29
 and culture, 118
 and humanism, 25
 and mysticism, 30
 and morality, 63-84

and politics, 115
and reason, 24
and society and culture, 108-136
definitions, 14
humanistic, 28
meaning, scope and implications, 9-33
meaning of, 11
primitive, 18
scientific study of, 113
role of in society, 114
theories of, 16
Rousseau, 80
Rowe, William, 54
Roy, M.N., 126
Royce, Josiah, 82, 96, 100, 103, 105
Russell, Bertrand, 126

**S**

Schleiermacher, 16
Science and technology, 125
Shaw, George Bernard, 15
Sin, evil effects of, 17
Socrates, 67, 87
Spinoza, 71
Stoics, 88
Supreme Being, 34, 36

**T**

Tennant, 137
Thomas, St., 89
Tillich, Paul, 9, 10, 14, 37
Toffler, Alvin, 126

**U**

Universal consciousness, 109
Unmoved mover, 34

**W**

Whitehead, A.N., 14, 19, 70, 80